# HAUNTED
## SOUTHWEST
## MONTANA

# HAUNTED
## SOUTHWEST
## MONTANA

DEBORAH CUYLE

Haunted
America

Published by Haunted America
A Division of The History Press
Charleston, SC
www.historypress.com

First published 2023

Manufactured in the United States

ISBN 9781467153683

Library of Congress Control Number: 2022950064

I dedicate this book to all of my friends, family and the team at Arcadia Publishing and The History Press. My love of history, writing and haunted places is fueled by their interest and support.

My appreciation also goes to all my spiritual BFFs who have joined me in a little ghost hunting now and then and have helped me pursue my paranormal research and beliefs. An open mind is an open door. I personally have experienced so many things I cannot explain that I can no longer even remotely doubt the existence of ghosts or spirits.

As I am currently living in a crumbling mansion built in 1883 (and also a former funeral home), I am discovering there are spirits everywhere—if we only take notice! We seem to have several friendly spirits entertaining us in this old house. So, I also dedicate this book to all the active ghosts out there. Without you, my books would not be possible!

*Happy ghost hunting!*

—Deborah Cuyle

# CONTENTS

Preface                                              9
Acknowledgements                                    13
Introduction                                        15

1. A Haunting History of Anaconda                   23
2. Anaconda Murders and Violence                    26
3. Haunted Hot Spots and Hotels                     50
4. Ghost Towns and Terrors                          58
5. Ghost Towns Nearby                               84
6. Pioneers Who Refuse to Leave                    100

In Conclusion                                      133
Bibliography                                       135
About the Author                                   143

# PREFACE

*Every city is a ghost. New buildings rise upon the bones of the old so that each shiny steel beam, each tower of brick carries within it the memories of what has gone before, an architectural haunting. Sometimes you can catch a glimpse of these former incarnations in the awkward angle of a street or filigreed gate, an old oak door peeking out from a new façade, the plaque commemorating the spot that was once a battleground, which became a saloon and is now a park.*
*—Libba Bray*

I hope readers visit many of these sites as they learn about the fascinating history of each of these haunted places. As is common with my books, I try to incorporate as many historical facts, names and dates as possible in each chapter. I feel this brings the ghosts and their stories to life and also makes learning about the towns more interesting. Many of my readers tell me they enjoy both—learning about the town's history *while* reading about the local spirits that haunt them. I love hearing a good ghost story, and then upon researching the building, I can actually find evidence of someone with the name of the spirit who actually lived there (or died there) at one time or another.

Being a NDE (near death experience) survivor, I am probably a little more open-minded than most people. Maybe someday science can prove what really happens to us after we die—the eternal mystery questioned by every living being—but until the riddle is solved, it is all just speculation. Religion and science may someday agree, but more likely, they will not. I see both sides of the debate. Too many unexplained things happen to each of us to not entertain the idea of ghosts and the spirit world. I read somewhere that God or spirits do give us signs when we ask for them, but we as humans are too busy or too close-minded to see them or recognize them. I often wonder what life would be like if people were not so skeptical of the possibility of the spirit world. How would that change the way people behave in this world today? Would this be reassuring or terrifying to most people? I am often baffled by people who tell me that they believe in the afterlife but not in spirits. How can the two really be separated? Perhaps some dead people just choose to haunt a place while other spirits choose not to? *A wonderful mystery.*

I have great interest and respect for the early pioneers, a fascination with local history and a personal passion for old buildings. I love all the lore, legends and ghost and spirit stories people have told me. It is fun to walk the same streets today—the same ones early settlers once walked—and think about how it was in the old days. When I look at old brick buildings or original hardwood floors, I try to imagine the thousands of people who once walked these streets or visited these buildings, the horses that pulled wagons and goods, the gunslingers and outlaws, the bartenders and shopkeepers, all of them living their lives and going about their business, just as we all do today. I would have loved to have been alive in the late 1800s.

History is full of people who haunt us, who want to be recognized and never forgotten for what they accomplished while alive, what improvements they created for a town or what they offered their family and community.

Ghost stories, legends and folklore exist in every town, big and small, new and old. Human beings are fascinated with the afterlife and are eager to somehow capture proof of the spirit world. But what are these spirits that people are so eager to find proof of? Apparitions and odors are the most common forms of paranormal activity, although odors are impossible to "capture" and prove the existence of. Strange noises are also common forms of paranormal activity. These noises often imitate the sounds of human, environmental and animal activities, such as crying and moaning, but they can also imitate the sounds of chairs moving or dishes breaking. Paranormal activity can also come in the form of a crisis apparition or the appearance of a passed loved one offering comfort. These are single events that typically occur when a living person undergoes a personal crisis. Unfortunately, these crisis apparitions are commonly shrugged off as daydreams or ignored and labeled as strange events caused by personal stress.

However, I would like for my readers to keep in mind how much energy it takes for a spirit to manifest itself. It is an extremely hard task, so it is very important that the spirit is acknowledged and given words of thanks. While single instances of paranormal activity are exciting, the apparition of an animal or a person is considered a haunting only when it continues to appear in the same location.

Within the walls of old buildings remains the residual energy needed to keep their spirits restless and their stories alive—and hopefully their ghostly apparitions seen today.

History is full of people who haunt us, who want to be recognized and never forgotten for what they accomplished while alive—the improvements they created for a town or what they offered their family and community. This book is about those fascinating spirits, the spirited people who made the places in *Haunted Southwest Montana* what they are today.

Most of the stories were told to me by locals, and some have been pulled from old newspapers—all told out of fun for the love of history and lore. This book is *not* intended to be a nonfiction project, and even after hundreds of hours hunched over reading and researching, I still find conflicting dates and inconsistent historic details, so please take it for what it is. I tried to be as accurate as possible with names, dates and details, but this is mostly a book full of tales of many mischievous ghosts and the interesting history of Anaconda and the nearby towns of southwest Montana. Enjoy!

# ACKNOWLEDGEMENTS

T here are many people to thank for this endeavor, and without their help and guidance, this book would not be possible. My wonderful editor, Artie Crisp, is always such a pleasure to work with, along with all the other incredible people at Arcadia Publishing and The History Press. Their mission to promote local history is passionate and infectious, and I am blessed to work on my books with them. Their dedication to recording local history is nothing less than amazing, and without them, many books would never be written.

My appreciation is extended to all those others who took the time to share with me their personal ghost stories and experiences. Without them, this book would not have the extra flair that I love so much!

And as always, I want to thank every single person who does what they can to preserve history—whether it is volunteering at the local historical society, maintaining old cemeteries and gravestones that otherwise would get neglected or simply researching their private genealogy through sites like Ancestry.com. In this fast-paced and high-tech world, the past can unfortunately be forgotten, and every effort to maintain and record valuable data, photographs, diaries, documents and records is of the upmost importance for future generations.

ONE FINAL REQUEST, *PLEASE do not disturb or trespass at any of the locations listed throughout this book without permission from the property or business owners,* as some have experienced property destruction, which is unfortunate. Although many of the buildings in *Haunted Southwest Montana* no longer exist, the energy left behind from a tragedy, murder or unsolved crime *does linger*. Please take only photographs back with you so the next person can have the same experience as you. Thank you for understanding.

# INTRODUCTION

*We're here, you know…all the time. You can talk to us and think about us.*
*It doesn't have to be sad or scary.*
—The Lovely Bones; *Susie Salmon, character; Alice Sebold, author*

*A*naconda: the word conjures images of large, slithering boas, their strength paralyzing and their presence intimidating and powerful. But the small town of Anaconda, nestled off I-90, is anything but intimidating. People are friendly, the businesses are noteworthy and the surroundings are both fascinating and beautiful.

Anaconda has, for 136 years, withstood destruction, violence, plagues, fires and financial disasters, proving how incredibly strong the city and its citizens are. The city is one of the ten oldest towns in Montana.

In 1886, the town had a population of just one thousand, and these residents lived mostly in small shacks at the end of the road nestled by the railroad tracks. The city was incorporated in 1888 and was supposed to be called Copperopolis but later was named Anaconda because there was already a town called Copperopolis. The name Anaconda was recommended by Mr. Clinton Moore, the United States postmaster general at the time.

In 1887, Anaconda had at least one dozen saloons that contributed to the town's loss of control, public drunkenness and escalating crime. Some of the guilty bars were G.R. McMillan Saloon, C.J. Collins Saloon, Jas Laundry and Saloon, Martin and Ramsey Saloon, Maud McLean Saloon, the McIlhenny Saloon, J.H. Bank Saloon and the Page and Stewart Saloon.

Hotel Montana was built in 1886 and located on Main Street. "The handsomest, most elegantly appointed hotel in the state, built in European style with strictly first-class cuisine and service." *Library of Congress, item no. 2017703025, John Margolies Roadside America.*

The Sweeney and Lawler Saloon was once located at 319 East Commercial Avenue in 1899. (It is the single-story building in the center.) It had a cast metal façade and pressed metal cornices. *Library of Congress.*

Montana became a state in 1889, and by 1900, over forty thousand people called Montana their home. Anaconda was becoming a growing concern, and people were beginning to take note of the beauty of the surrounding area and the rich possibilities within the mountains.

When Anaconda was thriving in the late 1890s, many shopkeepers sold their wares in town, countless bartenders peddled watered-down booze and flirty women plied the only thing some of them had to their name: their bodies.

Violence and lawlessness abounded in Anaconda. This kept the local undertakers, like Theo Ehret at 115 Main Street, very busy (phone number 29). Local business owners, such as D.G. Brownnell, who ran the livery stables on First Street if a horse needed new shoes, thrived. Another man, J.V. Collins, sold his famous table water, which he called "Idanha," that he brought in all the way from Soda Springs, Idaho, to sell in his shop at 521 East Park Avenue in Anaconda for eleven cents per bottle. Need a new pair of boots? Losee and Maxwell sold shoes in their shop located at 110 Main Street. Need a little help in the libido department? Head on out to D.M. Drug Company; they had a solution that promised to "restore manhood, nervous disorders, back pain, impotency and all its horrors that could make a man unfit to marry."

Gold was discovered near Anaconda by William Cummings on November 30, 1900, and this would soon start a rush of immigrants swarming to the area to claim their fortunes.

Some of the key players in Montana's local history were the bankers and mine owners. Marcus Daly (1841–1900) and his best friends for life James B. Haggin and M. Donahoe ran banks in Anaconda. The three leading "Copper Kings" were Marcus Daly, William Clark and Augustus Heinze.

Marcus Daly was born in 1841 to an Irish Catholic family. In 1856, at the young age of fifteen, he fled poverty and came to America in search of his dream.

He traveled from New York City to Salt Lake City, Utah, and then to Butte, Montana, in 1876. The local silver mines were being tapped out, so another revenue needed to be discovered. Daly was a brilliant man, and he also knew that the region's mountains held more than just silver—they were also filled with copper ore, ready for the taking. He quietly and effectively

Unidentified men leaving work at end of their shifts at the Anaconda Copper Mining Company smelter. *Library of Congress, item no. 2017837474.*

began purchasing every mine he could acquire and most of the land in Anaconda. Daly started the Anaconda Mining Company around 1880, and soon, the area nearby was termed the "richest hill on Earth." The little town of Anaconda was created to simply support his copper interests and smelter operation. Even with his enormous accumulation of wealth, Daly continued to be a working man without acting superior to those "below" him. He had a great reputation in town and was well liked by all (except his competing Copper Kings).

Daly purchased the Anthony Chaffin farmhouse in 1896 to build a summer home for his family. He would soon be busy remodeling the building until 1889 and then again in 1897 into the grand Queen Anne–style Victorian mansion now known as the Daly mansion. After Daly's death in 1900, his wife contacted architect A.J. Gibson to start another new look for the manor. This time, it would be a Georgian Revival–style home, which was finally completed in 1910. The Daly mansion has over fifty rooms, fifteen bathrooms and seven fireplaces and comprises twenty-four thousand square feet.

The imposing manor is located at 251 Eastside Highway in Hamilton, Montana, and some report that they have seen Daly's ghost roaming the grounds and hallways of his creation.

*Note: If you cannot travel to Montana to experience the beauty of the Daly Mansion in person, please enjoy their beautiful photographs online at https://www.dalymansion. org/tour/. There is also an audio tour online that describes each room in detail: https:// soundcloud.com/user-486048407-311710905/sets/daly-mansion-tour.*

In 1895, the Anaconda Company was the largest supplier of copper in the world.

Daly's fortune would grow even more in 1899, when he sold his company to Standard Oil for a whopping $39 million.

Daly's accomplishments in Anaconda were remarkable, and his imprint lives on today. Although he was buried at the Green-Wood Cemetery in New York City, many believe his spirit resides in his beloved hometown of Anaconda.

But newspapers echo tales of desperate gamblers and prospectors who risked everything in search of nearby copper and gold found deep within the hills of Bow County Valley and the Deer Lodge areas. Today, if the walls could talk in the buildings that still stand in the small towns that make up the valley, they would whisper dark tales of hushed murders, devastating fires and unfortunate mining conflicts.

The Daly Bank building, in 1895, was located at 123 Main Street in Anaconda. This image shows the original arched entrances when the building was home to Ossello's Appliance Store. *Library of Congress, item no. 100198p.*

John Benson met his fate at the hands of Charles Sheppard on a blustery, freezing night during the first week of November 1898. Sheppard struck Benson over the head with a chunk of fence pole, killing him. His body was finally found in January 1899, frozen in the water ten feet from the bank in Deer Lodge River. He had a deep wound at the base of his skull. Both men were working as section men for the railroad. They had been seen drinking together for two full days before Benson's disappearance, seemingly getting along fine. But somewhere along the way and multiple shots of whiskey and glasses of warm beer later, the two got into an argument while walking on the bridge. Only the killer and his victim know what the argument was really about. Once the ghastly deed was done, Sheppard hefted Benson's body up and threw it into the icy cold water below.

After a five-day trial, Sheppard was found guilty of murder in the second degree and sentenced to life imprisonment. One has to wonder if Benson's angry spirit still rests near the water's edge or if Sheppard's tortured soul still lingers within the confines of the prison's walls.

*Above*: Barich block (416–420 Park Street) was built in 1893 and originally housed a saloon and restaurant on the first floor and lodging accommodations on the second floor. *Library of Congress.*

*Right*: The Leader building at 121 Main Street was built in 1897. This image shows the building's fancy brickwork, beautiful and expensive copper embellishments and notable burglar alarm. *Library of Congress, item no. 2017703067; John Margolies, photographer.*

In the summer of 1917, a woman named Mrs. Nate Wheeler was murdered in cold blood in Anaconda. She was brutally shot while in the safety of her home in town. The police arrested Joseph Dilley after he confessed to the crime. The story unfolded that Mrs. Wheeler, an unnamed friend of hers and Dilley were out on a pleasure cruise in his car. Near the three-mile house, they lost control of the vehicle and damaged the car. The three ended up arguing over the damages. Wheeler, possibly drunk, ran back to her house and grabbed a gun. Dilley scuffled with Wheeler and shot her dead. Wherever the "three-mile house" was located, one could only assume that the restless spirit of the dead girl still lingers there, hoping to seek revenge on the man who ended her life over a dented bumper.

These ghosts and many others want their stories told as their restless spirits linger, twitchy for revenge, hopeful for acknowledgment or still searching for their long-anticipated mother lode of copper and gold.

Follow these stories from the smelters and buildings of Anaconda all the way to the area of Silver Bow and the Deer Lodge regions, where many unexplained ghosts and spiritual connections still linger more than one hundred years later.

# 1

# A Haunting History of Anaconda

*Maybe all the people who say ghosts don't exist are just afraid to admit that they do.*
—The Neverending Story, *Michael Ende*

Ghosts: a single word that conjures up all sorts of images and ideas about the spirit world. Hauntings and ghostly spirits have been around as long as humans and evoke every emotion from fear to intrigue and refusal of belief. Every culture treats death and the spirit world differently—different rituals, customs, burial practices—but all have one thing in common: the afterlife.

Ghost stories, legends and folklore exist in every town—big and small, new and old—as human beings are fascinated with the afterlife and are eager to capture proof of the spirit world. Apparitions are the most common form of paranormal activity. The spirit of an animal or a person that keeps reappearing at a location over and over again is classified as an actual haunting. An important characteristic of a classic haunting is noise. These noises imitate the sounds of human and animal activities, such as crying, chairs moving, dishes breaking or dogs barking.

Another form of activity is called the "crisis apparition." These are single paranormal events that typically occur when a living person undergoes a crisis and the spirit of a loved one appears to offer them comfort. These crisis apparitions are commonly shrugged off as daydreams or ignored and labeled as strange flukes caused by stress. With all the tragedies that Anaconda and nearby areas suffered, crisis apparitions would seem likely to occur there.

DEER LODGE COUNTY'S NEW COURT HOUSE AT ANACONDA.

The interior of the courthouse has a switchback staircase and a rotunda with hand-painted overhead dome frescoes. *From the* Anaconda Standard, *September 5, 1899.*

Old Montana State Prison was the site of a deadly riot and the murders of guards and inmates. Many restless spirits still roam the buildings. *Courtesy of Tananko, creative commons, Wikimedia.*

Anaconda, Montana, was once the paradise of three Copper Kings who made their fortunes mining the nearby mountains for ore. Marcus Daly established the town in 1883 and soon became rich beyond his wildest dreams when he built the smelter to process the copper. He built a mansion in nearby Hamilton, where his and his wife's spirits still roam the grand home.

Within the walls of the Copper Village Museum (the former city hall, jail and fire department of Anaconda), the ghosts of both a prisoner and fireman have been seen by many. Their phantom footsteps and paranormal activities have been frightening people since 1901. Fireman Jake Falk, afraid of nothing, begged five of his coworkers to stay the night in the building. By midnight, they were all certain the place was haunted.

Anaconda's famous ghost town and haunted bed-and-breakfast Gunslinger Gulch attracts thousands each year for a good dose of creepy research and nights full of frights. It is so haunted, it has earned its own series on the Discovery Channel called *Ghost Town Terror*. Plagued by an unsolved murder, angry prisoners and even the spirit of a dead cat, the owner and her family desperately seek help from paranormal experts.

The nearby area known as Deer Lodge has seen its share of violence in the past. In 1899, a drunken Charles Sheppard murdered John Benson with a fence post and then threw his body into the river. Some still witness the bloody apparition of a man at the water's edge. Just a year before Benson's murder, Michael Collins disappeared from Anaconda, his bloody garments found later by a passerby. Police never found his killer.

The old Montana State Prison, the first territorial prison in Montana, housed so many prisoners that within one month of being built, it was at full capacity. The prison still holds the residual energy from multiple executions, riots and violent deaths. Eerie shadow figures, unpleasant smells and feelings of dread are experienced by many who visit the old prison. Once, inmates took over the prison for thirty-six hours and killed three guards—their angry souls still seek revenge.

These true tales and many more can be found in *Haunted Southwest Montana*!

# 2

# ANACONDA MURDERS AND VIOLENCE

*Monsters are real. Ghosts are too. They live inside of us, and sometimes, they win.*
*—Stephen King*

Perhaps Anaconda and the surrounding towns are haunted due to the numerous intense murders and deaths from suicide that have occurred in the area. In the late 1890s, countless immigrants flooded into Anaconda and Deer Lodge Valley to work in the copper smelters. Almost every person in town worked in the smelter, and Anaconda flourished immensely between 1910 and 1920.

With the streets and saloons growing more crowded by the minute, it is no wonder tempers were quick and violence became commonplace. The long, exhausting and sweltering shifts of the workers drew them to the barstools of the saloons and the bedrooms of the brothels—to quench *both* thirsts.

Anaconda proprietor A.M. Walker ran the Commercial Hotel, located on the corner of Third and Main Streets, starting in 1895. He rented out rooms for two dollars a day and saw his share of crimes in town while running his lodgings. On March 14, 1895, Charles Brown shot Homer Hamilton in cold blood while chopping wood. In 1897, local faro dealer Billy Worley shot and killed a woman known as Blanche for not having a drink with him. That same year, John Bergen shot Bob Carr three times in town over a money dispute.

Many claim the souls of the citizens who were killed in Anaconda and the nearby shanty towns still roam the streets and buildings, unable to move on to the afterlife.

A view of Anaconda from the south, overlooking Main, Park and Commercial Streets, the central business district and the historic district. *Library of Congress, item no. 100165p.*

There is no way to discover and document all the killings that took place in the area, as many were never known about or simply went unsolved. It was common for the townspeople to truly *not care* whether a certain individual (whom no one liked anyway) was murdered. "He was an asshole, anyway. The world's better off without them," some said.

Back then, police had very little chances of clearing a homicide, as there typically were no valuable clues left behind. Officers had to piece together small bits of evidence, such as a footprint in the dirt, a crumpled sales receipt found nearby and missing shoes or clothes. There was no such thing as forensic science or labs.

Many feel the spirits of those who died tragically in Anaconda still roam the streets and haunt the buildings in town. Their trapped souls are eager to remain on Earth until their stories can be told or their killers finally punished.

# MAN'S BODY FOUND FROZEN IN THE RIVER

The bitter, freezing Montana winter can be unbearable for many people, and some suggest it can drive a person to madness. A man named William "Billy" Worley's life would change for the worse in February 1897. Worley killed his girlfriend Blanche Renaud at midnight on February 21 in the Badlands, and later, his body was found frozen solid at a river's edge. His body was located at the back end of the river, his throat slashed with a dull knife, cut from ear to ear.

When Deputies Corbett and Naughton retraced the dead man's footsteps for the evening, they discovered the story of the last few minutes of Worley's fatal night.

They began in the Shamrock Sporting House and then went down the embankment toward the river and across the ice. There, Worley was discovered facedown in the middle of the frozen stream, his head and shoulders stuck in the ice. The blood from his hastily slashed throat was solid, like chunks and threads from a red cloth slowly making their way downstream.

The police discovered that Worley was thirty-eight years old and that he sometimes dealt faro in Missoula, Montana. He had been harassing Blanche (whose real name was Marguerite Steeg) because she had fallen for a bartender named "Tex" who worked at the Office Saloon. Worley asked Blanche to have a beer with him, which she declined. This sent him into a rage, and he started shooting his revolver. The poor woman was shot multiple times. A local woman named Black Bessie went running out of the saloon, unfortunately also getting hit by a bullet, but it did no damage due to her steel corset.

Once Worley determined he had killed Blanche, he decided to turn the revolver on himself, but all of a sudden, he was a bad shot and did little more than put a few holes in his hat.

What happened to Worley next was a mystery until his body was found in the river. Worley had been seen everywhere from Missoula and Butte to Anaconda and all the towns in between.

Only eight women showed up for Blanche's service, one of the pallbearers being the man who made her killer red with jealousy.

No one took any interest in Worley's remains, so the county buried him in the potter's field. All he had to his name at the time of his death was a cheap watch.

Whether Worley's or Blanche's ghosts roam the local streets and pubs, no one really knows. If they do, perhaps the lovers' quarrel will go on for another century.

# The Anaconda Road Massacre

The year 1920 was a bloody one for the local miners. Tension was brewing, and arguments were heating up between the hardworking, underpaid copper miners and their bosses. As they watched the bigwigs build grand mansions and drive fancy cars, they struggled to make ends meet, despite working ten-hour shifts, as they made a paltry wage.

The miners felt a strike was in order. So on April 21, they began their picket lines at nearby Butte's Anaconda Copper Mining Company. The Metal Mine Workers Industrial Union teamed up with the Industrial Workers of the World (IWW) to demand higher wages and an eight-hour shift.

The morning of the strike, the angry men began blocking the roads that led to the mines. If any scabs (nonunion workers who cross picket lines) tried to cross the picket lines, they would be forced to turn back. The men held their ground, and by the next morning, most of the mines were empty, costing the mine owners plenty of money.

Alley, the manager of the Anaconda Copper Mining Company, was furious. "This strike will end immediately, or I will impose killings and hangings!" he yelled.

The strike continued. Soon, the guards were quickly deputized by the local sheriff, John K. O'Rourke.

But the tensions continued.

The next day, miners held fast to their posts, refusing to give in. Three hundred men (and several angry women) gathered together to show the strength behind their demands. As they huddled near the opening of the Neversweat Mine, they were determined to *not* back down. They firmly planted their feet on the Anaconda road just below the railroad tracks south of the High Ore Mine.

But the company's guards were ordered by Alley to shoot at the men. The shots blasted through the air, killing Thomas Manning and injuring sixteen other men. Manning suffered bullet wounds through his chest and stomach. It should be noted that all of the injured men were shot in their backs as they tried to run away.

To ward off any further violence, federal troops soon arrived.

Three weeks after the savage massacre, the men reluctantly returned to work.

Another miner who succumbed to his bullet wound was James Sullivan. Sullivan was a well-known miner in the Montana mining camps and the Coeur d'Alene region. Known by most as "Jimmie," he became crippled as a result of his wound. Doctors in Rochester, Minnesota, hoped they

An unidentified guard stationed at the lower gate at the Anaconda Copper Mining Company's smelter in 1942. *Library of Congress, item no. 2017837380; Russell Lee, photographer.*

could help Jimmie. More doctors in Chicago, Illinois, also felt they could give Sullivan relief. But nothing helped, and soon, Sullivan was shipped back to Ireland aboard a ship that was pulling out from New York Harbor. For a year, he struggled within the safety of his parent's home in Donaghadee, Ireland. After Jimmie's death, a cablegram was sent from Ireland to Butte to notify authorities of his demise. The cablegram read: "James Sullivan has succumbed to his wound, a bullet in his spine, fired there by one of the company's gunmen, with several hundred unarmed strike pickets fled down Anaconda hill to escape the rain of lead from the riot guns, rifles and revolvers of the company's gun-thugs and city policemen."

Sullivan was born in Spokane, Washington, and was twenty-seven years old at the time of his death. For twelve years before his death, he had been working in both Coeur d'Alene and Butte Mines.

At trial, the jury determined that the bullet that killed Manning was fired by an unknown person, so it could not be determined who was responsible.

Tom Manning's brutal and ruthless death went unpunished, and legend says that his angry spirit still seeks revenge.

*Note: The Anaconda Copper Mining Company had several different names over the years:*

*1880: The Anaconda Gold and Silver Mining Company*
*1891: The Anaconda Mining Company*
*1899: The Amalgamated Copper Company*
*1915: The Anaconda Copper Mining Company*
*1955: The Anaconda Company*
*1977: The Atlantic-Richfield Company (ARCO)*

# SERIAL KILLERS SHOEBOX ANNIE AND HER STEPSON, MAYER DECASTRO

*I heard stories about Shoebox Annie growing up in Anaconda.*
*How she would roam the streets selling miscellaneous junk.*
*I also heard how her and her son would kill people in town, then chop*
*them up and burn their body parts in the fireplace. Some people claim to*
*see her ghost, just an old lady really, still roaming the streets*
*of Anaconda looking for their next victim.*
*—Sue R.*

The residual energy of violent crimes and the restless spirits of those who commit them are often the reason places are haunted. And no two killers were more sinister in Anaconda's history than Mary Eleanor Smith, known as Shoebox Annie French, and her stepson, Mayer, who went by multiple aliases.

Some paranormal investigators feel that the ghosts of Shoebox Annie and her crazy son still roam the streets of Anaconda, Annie selling her miscellaneous wares stuffed into a small box and Mayer searching for their next victim.

Annie and her son lived in town in a brick house located on the north side of Alder Street at 643 (some records show 631) East Commercial Avenue. Annie got her nickname because she would wander through the town with an old shoebox filled with miscellaneous items to peddle—soap, buttons, shoelaces, combs, any little item she could put in her box that she might garner a penny or two. She also had a pet magpie that she trained to steal shiny objects. When Annie would go door to door to offer her wares, the bird would fly inside and grab small jewelry items, then just as quickly fly out of the house and back home.

The brick home soon developed a grisly reputation. People would sometimes go missing when they visited the French household. Annie's son, DeCastro Earl Mayer (also known as C.C. Skidmore and William Donald Mayer, Donny Mayer or C.D. Montaine), helped her carry out the gruesome task of killing their victims (either by poisoning or strangulation), soaking their bodies in a lye bath until the flesh fell off the bones, dismembering the bodies and then burning their remains in the fireplace. Although they later bragged about killing more people, they definitely killed four victims—even the local mailman went missing!

Supposedly, they would bury any leftover remains under their house in the depths of their basement. When police investigated, no remains were discovered.

Anaconda's serial killer Shoebox Annie was convicted of murder in 1938. She told the prison pastor, "I want to get right with my maker." She died in prison. *Washington State Archives, Corrections Department, Washington State Penitentiary, Commitment Registers and Mug Shots, 1887–1946.*

Locals avoided the house until the 1950s for fear of absorbing the bad energy left behind by the murders. (Note: the Frenches' house is no longer there.)

Mayer had a girlfriend who did not approve of his extracurricular activities in auto theft. Mayer was questioned by the police for several crimes. "She must have ratted you out," his mother warned him. "You better find her and talk to her." So, Mayer and his ex-girlfriend decided to meet up in Seattle to discuss matters, but he lost his temper. He assaulted the young girl, giving her two black eyes, and she had to go to the hospital in August 1920. As she was recovering in the hospital, Shoebox Annie and Mayer fled to Montana. This is when they settled and put roots down in Anaconda.

Their first known real victim was a man named Ole Larsen, who vanished while in Anaconda in 1921. Larsen had partnered up with Mayer in local oil deals. They had successfully sold some oil stocks together for $800. To celebrate their good fortune, Mayer invited Larsen over to his house for a fine, home-cooked meal made by his mother. Larsen was never seen again.

For two long days, locals complained about a putrid black smoke that was coming from the home on East Commercial Avenue as the son busied himself by chopping wood in the backyard. The son and his mother were seen driving around in Larsen's car, and oddly, the bank cashed a forged check for Annie for $750.

Meanwhile, Mayer sweet-talked his Texan girlfriend, now healed from his attack, to move to Anaconda from Seattle. He wanted the three to live together as a family. For some reason, the girl agreed and was soon living in Montana. She had been living there for only a couple of weeks when the tell-tale black smoke began billowing from the chimney once again. The unnamed girl was also never seen again.

Sheriff J.J. Murphy from nearby Butte was called to investigate the case of the missing girl. When he arrived, he noticed Annie was wearing a dress that was much too young for her, along with some jewelry that seemed out of place. Meanwhile, Mayer was busy selling some of the victim's other pieces of jewelry at the local pawn shop. The frustrated sheriff, although certain there had been foul play, was unable to conclude that the girl had fallen at the hands of Shoebox Annie and Mayer. Since there was no body to be found (a situation known as corpus delicti), charges could not be filed against Mayer or his mother.

The young girl's worried mother was not all right with this outcome. She angrily traveled to Anaconda to search for and hopefully rescue her daughter. Upon the woman's arrival at the French house, her daughter was not there. The mother lost her mind and shot Annie. But Annie never went to the police to file charges against the mother.

Later, Shoebox Annie and her stepson admitted to killing a woman named Mrs. Abel LaCasse for profit in 1921. She was robbed of two diamond rings and a diamond watch. It is unclear whether this woman was one of Mayer's girlfriends. The pair confessed that they shot her while she was asleep in their home, dismembered her and then buried her body in a ditch somewhere between Anaconda's smelter stack and Warm Springs. Her body parts were never located. The poor victim had been a schoolteacher in Butte, Montana, before her untimely demise.

Sensing that the police were close on their tails, Annie and Mayer decided to leave town and let things cool down for a bit. They sold a car to a man in Anaconda for $365. But when the man took the car to a garage for repairs, the serviceman discovered the vehicle's numbers had been altered, which typically meant the car was stolen. And it had been stolen from a woman in Salt Lake City.

When the sinister duo was staying in Idaho, the police in Pocatello learned of their criminal activity. The sedan they were driving was stolen. When the police arrived at the location where Mayer was staying, they snuck up on him. He was carrying a rifle, a bag of stolen plates, phony driver's licenses and wire snippers. He was promptly arrested. Back at the station, as Mayer was getting out of the police wagon, he quickly tried to make a break for it. The situation escalated into an aggravated arrest, and Mayer found himself at the wrong end of a bullet. He was shot in the shoulder and forearm. Somehow, he managed to get away.

The police drove back to Mayer's residence, hoping to find him there. Sure enough, Mayer was in the garage, furiously attempting to switch out plates on the car and bleeding all over the floor as he was doing it. He was handcuffed again. Inside the house, there was evidence of bootlegged whiskey, and Annie was also arrested.

Once Mayer was in the hospital in Pocatello, Officer Tom Roan sat by his bedside to guard him. He tried to get Mayer to talk by tricking him: "You know, they found the bones of that girl you killed," he said.

While Mayer was lounging in a hospital bed being given the best care, he was questioned about the missing girl.

"You will never find her," he said coldly.

Mayer was sent to Utah on a stolen automobile charge; he got a twenty-five-dollar fine and was sentenced to ten years in prison. (He was also wanted on charges in California, Washington, Montana, Colorado, Kansas, Utah and Idaho.) His mother played the "poor us" card, sobbing profusely again in front of the parole board, and again, Mayer was released early, after just three years. But he was arrested almost as soon as he was released for stealing furniture in Colorado. Then he pulled a stunt in Idaho that caused him to go back to jail on larceny charges. Once behind bars, on Halloween night, Mayer and seven other prisoners (including two female inmates) managed to break out. Mayer was caught again and sent to Leavenworth State Prison in Kansas on white slavery (human trafficking) charges.

Meanwhile, Shoebox Annie decided she needed to find a new avenue to make money. In 1926, she decided to marry a seventy-two-year-old man in Seattle. The ink was not even dry on their marriage certificate when Annie took out a life insurance policy on him. Annie was known to talk in her sleep and spoke of her plans one night while slumbering. The new groom heard of her plans to kill him and immediately demanded she leave his house.

In 1928, another naïve man, Lieutenant James Eugene Bassett, arrived in Seattle, Washington. He was an officer in the navy, so living near the base in Seattle was convenient. Bassett decided he would no longer need his blue Chrysler sports roadster, as his next assignment was in the Philippines, so he put an advertisement in the newspaper offering it for sale. On October 16, Mayer offered Bassett $1,600 for his car. "But I will want a trial drive first, of course," Mayer told Bassett. "Say we motor out to the suburbs. We will take my elderly aunt along because she is putting up the cash for me." Soon, Mayer and his mother were off to Washington to "purchase" the car.

The three drove the auto around the streets of Bothell, Washington, and since the roadster was running in tip-top shape, the deal was sealed. They finished the trip in a little brown house in Bothell, where Bassett would meet his maker.

No money would ever change hands, and Bassett was never seen again, just like Larsen. When Bassett neglected to show up to board his ship on Monday, a call was made for his disappearance. Possibly, his superiors in the Office of Naval Intelligence thought he was just going AWOL (absent without official leave). Perhaps he was suffering from the anxiety of his recent move to Washington from Maryland. Yet Bassett had no history of anxiety, depression or bad work ethics. Something was terribly wrong. An APB (all-points bulletin) was issued for Bassett by the Seattle Police Department.

A week later, Oakland, California police officers had his roadster pulled over, and Shoebox Annie and her son were driving it. Mayer said he had no idea what happened to Bassett. In the car's trunk, police found many suspicious items: rope, chloroform, a gas gun, a rifle with an attached silencer and heavy tongs (used for breaking bones). Mayer also had Bassett's watch, wallet and cufflinks in his possession. But was this enough evidence to convince a jury? Mayer's fingerprints were taken and supplied to the FBI. Mayer was arrested on automobile theft charges. Later, it was said that Mayer had savagely killed Bassett with a hammer and then scattered his dismembered remains all over northern King County, Washington, in the little towns of Bothell, Cathcart and Woodinville. State Police Chief William

Shoebox Annie at the age of seventy-three and her stepson, Mayer, when they were arrested for grand larceny. He died by suicide while serving out his sentence. *Washington State Archives, Corrections Department, Washington State Penitentiary, Commitment Registers and Mug Shots, 1887–1946.*

Cole and his men desperately searched the Bothell area for a solid eighteen months, leaving no stone unturned, in search for Bassett's body, but it was never found.

Mayer's mother cried in front of his parole board and made up a good story about how good her son was and how they were just poor. Strangely, after much overexaggerated sobbing from his stepmother, Mayer was released.

Eventually, in 1930, sixty-five-year-old Annie was arrested and thrown into jail for grand larceny charges and became Washington State Prison inmate no. 13327. She was released early, completing only part of her five-year sentence. In 1938, she was convicted of murder in the first degree at the age of seventy-three and became inmate no. 17703 after being sentenced to life in prison. State Patrolman Joe McCauley disguised himself as a priest to obtain information from Shoebox Annie about the murders. She told the prison pastor in confidence, "I want to get right with my maker." She eventually died in prison. McCauley later testified, "It was the toughest and weirdest assignments I have ever undertaken. I dressed in clergyman's clothes, and no one in prison except the warden knew anything about the deception."

Mayer was not as fortunate as his stepmother. The court system considered him a habitual offender and gave him life imprisonment. He became inmate no. 12444 in 1929, also at Washington State Prison. He died by suicide while serving out his sentence.

The pair also confessed to killing a man known as Dave Randall and said that they buried his body in a stone quarry somewhere near Pocatello, Idaho.

Shoebox Annie and Mayer were ruthless killers who terrified Anaconda locals while living there—and for decades after. Three people vanished while conducting business with them between 1917 and 1928. Three more individuals went missing, too—and were never found. Out of all the tortures they instilled on people who were strangers or simply became involved in their lives, it is unimaginable that they got away with murder for decades. Some considered their crimes to be the perfect murders.

No murder is perfect—it may just take a little longer to catch the killers.

Are the restless spirits of Shoebox Annie and her son, Mayer, still roaming the streets of Anaconda near East Commercial and Alder Streets, looking for their next victim? For decades, many people could not gather the courage to even walk past the old brick house where several people were brutally murdered. Does the area where the old brick home once stood still hold any residual energy?

## HORSE RACES AND A MURDER

Around August 1899, a man named John Bray killed his partner and friend James Hayes at the racetrack in Anaconda. Bray was a well-liked and well-known cowboy who specialized in racehorses, and everyone seemed to know Bray at every racetrack in Montana. He was born around 1870 (other documents state he was born in 1866, but back then, identification was not the same as it is today, and many pioneers had no idea how old they were or when they were actually born) and came to Montana from Corning, New York, in 1879. He moved to California for a few years in 1885 and then came back to Montana. Bray was just twenty-nine years old when he and Hayes went to Butte, Montana, together to gather some horses. They were going to bring some horses back with them through Racetrack and Deer Lodge and then head on over to Anaconda.

After Hayes's murder and Bray's imprisonment, Bray was interviewed by the *Anaconda Standard* in late December 1899. He calmly told of the trouble he had gotten himself into:

> *On the night of the trouble, I had been out of town and came back to the racetrack in a hack. I went to the judges' stand, where the saloon was, and*

In August 1899, a man named John Bray killed his partner and friend James Hayes at the racetrack in Anaconda. *From "Eager for the Race" by Louis Maurer (New York: Currier & Ives, circa 1893); courtesy of Library of Congress, item no. 92510117.*

*the man that ran the peanut stand told me that the saloon had closed up and he could not get his blankets. He asked me if I had blankets, and I said I had some over in the stall. He said that I had better get them and come over and make a bed with him. I went over and got the blankets, and when I came back, I met Hayes. In the meantime, the saloon had reopened, and the man who ran the peanut stand had gotten his blankets.*

He continued, "A man from Denver had a bottle of whiskey, and we took a drink. We had some tomatoes and peanuts, and Hayes said, 'Let's go over to the stall, there is a keg of beer there.' I took my blankets over with Hayes to sleep with him. When I got over to the stall, there were White, Munch, Brown, Perry, O'Malley, Foye, Knapp and a few others. We were all drinking."

The long night seemed to take a sinister turn, one that would change the men's lives forever.

Hayes remembered the men finishing off one keg, going to town and getting a second keg to share. They drank that up and then another. Hayes then told Bray, "I expect there was going to be a new jock to take charge of my stable in the morning. My boss thinks there is too much beer around here."

"I do not need your job. I have a better one already," Bray told Hayes. Then Hayes suggested they fight. "There is no money in fighting."

But Hayes was already fired up and boasted he could lick Bray in five minutes or less. The men had been drinking all day and night. The next morning, the drinking continued, even as they harnessed and tacked up the horses. Bray's memory failed him from all the beer and whiskey. The next thing he knew, he was locked up in the county jail, hungover. When he asked why he was in jail, the warden told him, "You cut up Knapp and killed a few men at the racetrack in Anaconda."

It did not take long for the jury to convict poor old Bray. In just four hours, they passed the verdict of manslaughter. Bray was sentenced to one to ten years in prison for crimes he did not even remember committing.

## Anaconda's Ex-Mayor Kills a Man in Cold Blood

Many hauntings begin with the simple fact that a murder was never solved or resolved. When a spirit remains on Earth, taunting those around it, it is

FRED GAGNER

Anaconda's ex-mayor Fred Gagner murdered his friend Fred Anderson on November 2, 1921, over rent. Gagner was sentenced to a mere thirty days behind bars and given a $150 fine. *From the* Butte Miner, *November 3, 1921.*

typically seeking a resolution for its untimely death. Does the ghost seek revenge? Does the ghost want its killer to be slain, too? Or does the ghost desire something else?

In the case of Fred Gagner versus Fred Anderson, it's possible that the spirit of Anderson is still angry about his death and the minimal punishment his cold-blooded killer was sentenced to.

On the cold night of November 2, 1921, two men's lives were changed forever—one man's spirit may still haunt Anaconda.

The day started out as usual. Then by evening, things took a turn for the worse.

Fred Gagner and John Anderson had been friends for twenty-eight years. Both had emigrated from Sweden. Gagner was an ex-police officer, and Anderson was a harness maker. Anderson had worked on Gagner's ranch for seven years and had rented a cabin by the Lakeside Inn from him for five years. Anderson wanted to be closer to the mine where he worked, so he moved out. On November 2, 1921, he had just come back to the small cabin to pick up the last of his personal belongings.

The tension started because Gagner believed Anderson still owed him some rent. Anderson felt Gagner still owed him for some work he had done on the ranch. "He only paid me with five gallons of moonshine," Anderson later stated on his deathbed.

Gagner, after a few whiskeys, marched down to the cabin to confront Anderson. The two got into a pissing match, and although the truth was never really known, Gagner stated that his revolver fell out of his pocket and went off when it hit the ground. The stray bullet *accidentally* hit Anderson.

After the scuffle, Gagner marched back to his cabin a few miles away and went to bed.

Anderson lay down in his own bed, bleeding. A few neighbors came over to check on him. They saw the bullet wound, and Nels Pearson immediately went to the closest farm that had a phone. "Gagner shot Anderson," he told Anaconda sheriff C.L. Beal. Soon, Beal and his deputy Osborne were making their way to Gagner's house.

"We need to arrest you," they told him.

"You got a warrant?" Gagner snapped.

"No, but you need to come along. You are under arrest for shooting John Anderson."

"If you ain't got a warrant, then I will see you at the police station in the morning," he said.

The men agreed.

Gagner was not a stranger to Anaconda. Born in Sweden, he had resided in Montana for thirty-eight of his sixty-three years. In 1894, he became a police officer for Anaconda, and in 1902, he became a member of legislature. In 1909, he became the mayor of Anaconda and remained in the postition until he purchased his farm five years prior to the murder. He was well respected and liked in the community. He was not perfect though; he had prior charges against him for bootlegging liquor during Prohibition. This landed him a $150 fine for the liquor violation and thirty days in jail.

Anderson was rushed to St. Ann's Hospital in town, where he was treated for his gunshot wound.

Gagner was arrested on first-degree murder charges and was sitting in the county jail with a $15,000 bail hanging over his head.

Neither the measly amount of rent nor the little amount of money due for a small job could possibly be worth the trouble brewing for both of the men now.

Anderson lay in his bed, knowing his time to meet his maker was coming soon. He summoned several people to make his deathbed statement. He proclaimed Gagner shot him for no good reason. His dying statement was written as follows:

*I, John Anderson, believing myself about to die, and under the fear of death make this statement as to how I received the wound that is causing my death.....A little before 7 o'clock p.m. on the evening of Wednesday, November 2, 1921, I was in one of Fred Gagner's cabins at Georgetown Lake, Deer Lodge County, when Fred Gagner, accompanied by Jim Norton, came to the cabin and demanded that I pay the rent due....I told him I would not do so until he paid me for the work I'd done....The last thing I'd got from him was five gallons of moonshine. "Is that the reason you don't think you have to pay the cabin rent?" he said. Gagner got mad; then he said he thought he would kill me, and I replied it would not be that much to kill. Fred Gagner then shot me once and turned around and walked out of the cabin.*

*I called to Jim Norton to help me into bed, and he would not come back. The bullet from Gagner's gun hit me in the shoulder, and I was unable to move any part of my body except my right arm. After Gagner and Norton left, Fred Smith came to the cabin and picked me up and put me in bed. John Lyons came with Fred Smith. It is a true and correct statement of the shooting of me by Fred Gagner.*

*Dated Nov. 2, 1921. St. Ann's Hospital, Anaconda, Montana.*

*John* [his X mark] *Anderson* [followed by the signatures of six people]

With such a statement and multiple witnesses, one would think the case would be a slam dunk.

Nothing could have been further from the truth.

John Anderson (1854–1921) expired at 9:00 p.m. on November 2 at the hospital, a nurse at his side. His last dying words were, "Gagner shot me." He was sixty years old. The coroner's inquest was scheduled for the following Monday at 7:30 p.m. at a room inside Tuttle's Undertaking.

Four different doctors performed autopsies: Dr. A.J. Willits, Dr. W.E. Long, Dr. John Noonan and Dr. T.J. McKenzie. The high-profile case garnered much local attention, and the facts and details had to be well documented. No mistakes that the lawyers could use against Anderson could be made. All four doctors agreed that a single bullet had entered Anderson's left shoulder, went through his lung and out through his back, causing paralysis. The hemorrhaging was the result of a gunshot wound.

Anderson was buried at the Upper Hill Cemetery in Anaconda.

It is interesting to note that Gagner ended up having *four* trials, and his prosecution seemed to drag on forever. He pleaded not guilty and continued to defend his innocence, determined that the gun misfired accidentally as he went to kick Anderson.

Finally, on October 28, 1923, Fred Gagner pleaded guilty to the charges. His punishment? A mere thirty days behind bars and $150 fine, plus court costs. His court costs? The first trial cost $784.35, the second $1,137.45, the third $2,761.55 and the fourth and final $1,413.91. It seems that it would have been smarter for Gagner to just walk away from his few dollars' worth of missed rent.

And no one could blame poor old Anderson for wanting to haunt Anaconda. Justice was definitely *not* served. Gagner got the same fine and number of days in jail for bootlegging as he did for brutally taking Anderson's life over a few bucks.

It is possible that Anderson still roams the streets of Anaconda, searching for Gagner so he can take out revenge on him.

# MURDER AT WASHOE NEW WORKS SMELTER

The Washoe Works Company in Anaconda was a very profitable business. In 1898, it was reported in the *Anaconda Standard* that in one year, the company had produced 1,459,249 tons of raw ore that had been brought from Butte to be processed in the Anaconda smelter. In that, 124,418 pounds of copper had been produced, 5,074,036 ounces of silver had been extracted and 135,244 ounces of gold had been drawn. The works had spent $150,000 on powder used and another $41,761 on candles. Its total profits in one year were a whopping $22.5 million.

Another murder was committed in town on July 19, 1902, leaving William Evans (1840–1902) dead. Does his angry and restless spirit still roam the area?

Evans was one of Montana's most prominent citizens at the time of his demise. He was the superintendent of machinery at the smelter. John McGeary carried anger in his mind for Evans and was determined to kill him. His motive was revenge.

Four days before the tragedy, McGeary purchased a gun for $4.75 at a local pawn shop on Main Street. The proprietor M. Millzner told the man that he would have to come back to pick up the weapon, since it was after 6:00 p.m. McGeary agreed and said he would return.

Once he had the gun in his possession, McGeary planned his next move. The morning of the murder, McGeary waited for his opportunity as he hid behind the buggy shed. When he saw Evans walking by, he quickly drew his pistol and shot at his target. Evans suffered a bullet wound to his right side by his liver and a second bullet punctured the back of his neck. "I am even with you now!" shouted McGeary.

William Gerard, the assistant engineer at Washoe New Works Smelter on the outskirts of Anaconda, was a witness to the murder. "The shooting was at 9:00 a.m. I looked out the window after I heard the first shot. Then I saw McGeary after the second shot; he was about thirty feet from the stable with a gun in his right hand."

McGeary attempted to make a run for it, but he was quickly pursued by C.I. "Doc" Emerson and E.A. Waterbury, who galloped after the murderer, pursuing him all the way to the bicycle shed as he headed toward Anaconda. McGeary may have been trying to make his way back to his home at 416 East Fourth Street, where he lived with his family. The two heroes shot at McGeary with their rifles until he surrendered. Once in custody, McGeary was handed over to Sheriff Morgan to be taken to the county jail.

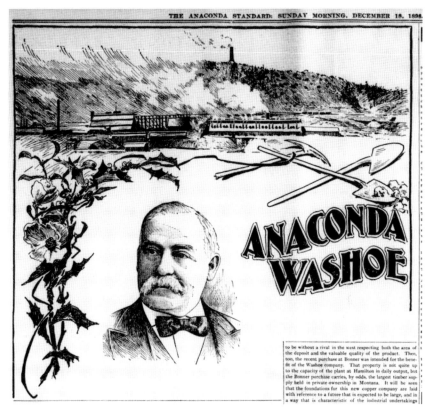

THE ANACONDA STANDARD: SUNDAY MORNING, DECEMBER 18, 1898.

ANACONDA WASHOE

to be without a rival in the west respecting both the area of the deposit and the valuable quality of the product. Then, too, the recent purchase at Bonner was intended for the benefit of the Washoe company. That property is not quite up to the capacity of the plant at Hamilton in daily output, but the Bonner purchase carries, by odds, the largest timber supply held in private ownership in Montana. It will be seen that the foundations for this new copper company are laid with reference to a future that is expected to be large, and in a way that is characteristic of the industrial undertakings

Marcus Daly with the Washoe Company in the background. William Evans was murdered by John McGeary. The motive was revenge. *From the* Anaconda Standard, *December 18, 1898.*

It came to the surface that McGeary was angry that Evans did not take his improvement for a device that was to be used in the converters seriously.

Before dying, Evans gave a signed statement about what happened that fateful morning, and it was printed in the *Butte Miner* on July 20:

> *I, William John Evans, knowing that I cannot live and having no hope of living, hereby declare that the defendant, John McGeary, told me this morning that the concentrator was no good and wished to know why I did not adopt his improvement. I told him to go to the concentrator superintendent and the foreman, and any arrangement made by and with them would be satisfactory. I turned away and went towards the office when he fired the first shot, and as I lay on the ground, he shot me again. I dropped when the first shot took effect. I cannot say where. I had no weapon with me.*

Evans died at ten o'clock that night. He was born in Scotland and came to America in 1859 to start a new life when he was just nineteen years old. He made his way to Montana in 1887 and then to Anaconda in 1899. One of the reasons Evans may have not wanted McGeary to pursue a new patent on his invention was because he was the patentee of the Evans round table that was used everywhere in the concentrators in smelters. Would McGeary's new design have risked Evans? It is highly probable that the animosity between the men was purely based on money. Evans was financially secure, whereas McGeary was still a struggling working teenager. McGeary had also gotten hurt at the smelter and was seeking damages, which he never received.

W.E. Esterbrook, the superintendent of the concentrator at Washoe New Works in Anaconda, testified, "I have been connected to concentrators for eighteen years, and so far as I can tell, the rack of the defendant was really practical and could have been used with some satisfaction."

After the long, drawn-out task of securing a jury, the trial dragged on for several days. Eventually, McGeary was sentenced to twelve years of hard labor at Montana State Penitentiary.

Who knows, maybe the two men are still battling over smelter concentrators in the afterlife.

# A Claim Jumper Meets His Maker

Claim jumping was a very risky business, and most who performed this unlawful act were often murdered by the claims' rightful owners. Claim jumping was a term used by miners to describe when a person works a claim that another person owns the rights to. Basically, it's stealing.

If a miner was found working a claim unlawfully, many times, he was shot on the spot or hanged from the nearest tree.

One such sad soul met his fate on the cold night of January 7, 1899.

There were no clues left at the scene, leaving the local Anaconda sheriff scratching his head.

The corpse was discovered by Henry Gallahan around noon the day after the murder. The body lay in a drift of snow about fifty feet from the Britannic Mine near Hall's Ranch in town, over near the city dump on Rocker Road. The body had been butchered almost beyond recognition.

Gallahan ran, terrified, to Clark's farm, which had the only personal telephone in Anaconda at the time. He notified the police of the grisly discovery.

Coroner Jullien showed up with Sheriff Murphy to investigate the scene. The man had suffered two deep gashes to his head, and by the looks of it, they were caused by a miner's pick. The body was lying in a pool of blood. The victim had an old Mastiff plug cut chewing tobacco pouch on him that he had been using as a coin purse. Inside was ninety-five cents. Between the victim's sprawled legs was a single footprint in the snow and a half-dozen burned matches. Obviously, the killer smoked.

The men followed the trail of bloody snow about fifty yards back toward the road. There, they came upon a gruesome site: bits of brains and more blood. There were also a few handprints in the snow. It looked as if the victim was killed near the road and then his body had been dragged down in the hopes of hiding it.

The coroner noted that the unknown man was about five feet, ten inches tall, weighed around 180 pounds and had brown hair and a moustache. He was approximately thirty-five years old. His shoes were also missing (but that was a common thing back then, as shoes were expensive).

Back at the mortuary in Anaconda, over one thousand people came to view the cleaned-up body, compliments of the local undertaker Mr. Tachell. A few people thought they recognized the poor man. Some felt it was George Pearson, a blacksmith from Eureka, Nevada, who had come to Butte and Anaconda for a visit. He had been seen drinking at the Silver Bow Brewery on Main Street just two days before. Others suggested the deceased was a prospector, due to the fact that his pocket held a piece of candle and the wounds had been inflicted by a miner's pick. Perhaps he was a claim jumper who just got his due.

No one will ever know the true identity of the bludgeoned man.

He is just one more lost soul in Anaconda's violent history who perhaps still haunts the town.

## SIMPLE SALOON BRAWL LEADS TO MURDER

On a crisp April night in 1904, cold beer was being tossed back by locals in Anaconda at one of the local pubs. But soon, the night turned deadly.

Nineteen-year-old George Dimich wanted no trouble. He just wanted to enjoy a few beers in peace and quiet as he sat on a barstool at Ignace Miller's Cash Saloon at 723 East Park Avenue on the eastern side of the small town. A stranger sauntered up to where Dimich was sitting and asked if he wanted to fight.

"I do not want to fight," Dimich calmly told him. He casually moved away to the other side of the bar. Soon, six Swedes surrounded the man, one quickly pulling out a chair out and lifting it to hit Dimish over the head. In defense, Dimich drew his jacket knife and waved it at the strangers. As one of the men, Chris Halstead, came at him, Dimich felt the knife go into his side. Dimich and his two friends, Raidacovich and Vucmanovich, ran out of the bar. They ran out into the street and tried to make their way back to their cabin.

Halstead knew he had been stabbed. He stumbled his way out into the street, blood dripping on the floor as he walked. When he was in the street, Halstead started to feel faint. He was losing blood and could feel that he had been stabbed at least two times. A hack was summoned to haul the injured man to nearby St. Ann's Hospital.

Halstead received treatment for his wounds, but the doctor was doubtful the man would survive.

On his deathbed, Halstead told police, "I was down in an Austrian saloon….I was asked to take a glass of beer; then some fellow hit me."

The officer Frank Petelin asked him, "Do you believe you are going to die?"

"I do not know; I hope so. I am not sure of it yet."

"How did the fight start?"

"He called my partner a son of a bitch, and three fellows came for me. The first one hit me with a knife, and another took a chair and hit my partner. This was in the saloon. I never hit anybody."

Halstead succumbed to his wounds the next day.

Dimich was only a teenager who barely spoke English, and Norway native Halstead was just twenty-four years old. Coroner Walsh hauled the dead man's body back to the morgue. Halstead had received a fatal knife would in his tenth rib, and this caused internal damage and bleeding.

Dimich pleaded not guilty to the charge of manslaughter.

The parcel where Ingace Miller's Cash Saloon once stood on Park Avenue is now a vacant lot.

Some could warrant that the residual energy where the blood drained the life from Halstead's body might hold negative impressions. Does Halstead's ghost roam Park Avenue, seeking revenge for his untimely murder?

No one really knows.

# Killer Dan Lucey Blames the *Anaconda Standard* for His Hanging

Dan Lucey would be a great candidate for deciding to haunt Anaconda and nearby Butte. On the gallows, his final words were, "I was convicted through prejudice worked up by the *Anaconda Standard* and the city's attorney Connolly!"

Lucey was angry at everyone who wrote an article about his crimes and published them in the newspaper. He did not feel he got a fair trial. (Although, he confessed to killing Patrick Reagen right before he was hanged on September 2, 1898. He even wrote the strange confession down with a pencil and signed and dated it.) Lucey felt the crime should have been considered a homicide, not a murder. His handwritten statement did little to help his case:

> *If I should hang, I know that the people will say that I am guilty, and I might as well confide my secrets to some friend.…I don't believe there is much hope for me, but if I should get off, what I now tell you is never to be mentioned under penalty of death. I am not guilty of murder in the first degree, but I killed Pat Reagan all right, but he was my friend and I did not intend to and accused me of having it kill him when the trouble commenced.*
>
> *We had some drinks and kept drinking all the time, and we both got pretty full. I guess we kept going until about midnight. Reagan lost some money and accused me of having it. I said something to him, and he struck at me with a rock. I struck him with my other fist, and we both got down together. He got another rock and was trying to beat me with it when I got ahold of the rock and I hit him over the head twice with it. I guess I must have killed him then, for he did not speak after that.*
>
> *I was scared and did not know what to do, and being drunk, I thought the best thing to do was get rid of the body.*
>
> *I could hear the water running in the creek, so I took the body and put it in the creek.*
>
> *I started back toward Anaconda on the track. As I passed the place where we had the fight, I looked for Reagan's body and could not find it. By this time I was about sober.…I went on to a saloon. I woke up, and me and the saloonkeeper had quite a few drinks.*

Later, in jail, Lucey also told other prisoners that he and Reagan were headed to British Columbia together but got in a fight. He said he hit his

PATRICK L. REAGAN.

*Left*: Dan Lucey hid out in Anaconda after brutally and mercilessly killing Patrick Reagan. Some say they both still haunt the town. *From the* Anaconda Standard, *February 3, 1901.*

*Right*: Patrick Reagan was murdered in 1901. "Reagan was one of the most cold-blooded man that ever walked the Earth! Why, even his closest friends are afraid of him!" said Lucey. *From the* Anaconda Standard, *February 3, 1901.*

head with a rock and then threw him in the river. "Reagan was one of the most cold-blooded men that ever walked the Earth! Why, even his closest friends are afraid of him!" said Lucey.

Hoping for a little sympathy, Lucey offered the judge the fact that he knew who killed a man named Ogle in Belgrade, Montana. This was of interest to the officers because Ogle was a Northern Pacific Railroad station agent, not a hoodlum. Ogle was murdered in 1894, and his killer was never discovered.

On July 16, 1900, the Supreme Court denied Lucey a new trial. He was hanged in Butte on September 14, 1900.

Ever since Lucey's hanging, many locals have claimed to see his ghostly image haunting buildings, streets and fields around town. His apparition has been seen by many locals in areas such as Anaconda, Butte, Silver Bow Canyon and even as far away as Centerville (near Great Falls, Montana). It has appeared many times on the banks near the BA&P Railroad tracks near Bow Canyon River. Lucey's ghost is always wearing a long, black robe. It was rumored that Dan Lucey, while alive, stayed in Anaconda because he felt safer there than he did anywhere else.

The *Anaconda Standard* received so many calls about the ghost that it finally wrote feature on it:

> *A dozen ghost hunters have called the* Standard *and related alleged meetings with the monster who, contrary to ghostly traditions, persists in clothing himself in a long, black robe. Two men declared that they met and talked with the ghost Thursday night in another part of the city, and they assert the apparition posed as the departed spirit of Dan Lucey, who was hanged here several months ago for the murder of Patrick Reagen, in Silver Bow Canyon. Others declare with a solemness that almost makes an impression upon the non-believer that they have encountered his ghostly majesty, and the various experiences are both interesting to listen to and amusing.*
> —Anaconda Standard, *March 17, 1901.*

If Lucey harbored resentment and anger right before his neck snapped on the gallows, it would make sense that his ghost still roams the area, pointing its boney, skeletal finger at someone else to blame for his crime.

# 3

# HAUNTED HOT SPOTS AND HOTELS

*Now I know what a ghost is. Unfinished business, that's what.*
*—Salman Rushdie*

## ANACONDA'S OLD CITY HALL: THE COPPER VILLAGE MUSEUM

One of the most notorious haunted locations in Anaconda is Anaconda's old city hall, now the Copper Village Museum, Historical Society and an active arts center located at 401 East Commercial Street. In the late 1800s, locals (along with Marcus Daly) hoped Anaconda would become the state capital. Due to this expectation, the brick building was quite lavish. Completed in 1896, it is still a landmark today. It used to contain city government offices, the city jail, the city police department and even the city fire department. One can even view the old jail cells in the basement of the building, which is now part of the historical society.

The basement and a section of the main floor are now the Marcus Daly Historical Museum, which offers the viewing of many old artifacts from Anaconda's mining era. The building has gone through some challenging phases; in 1974, the clock tower and fire bell were removed, and then in 1976, it was scheduled for demolition. Luckily, it was rescued by concerned citizens (led by Alice Clark Finnegan) in 1978, with the help of a grant from the National Trust for Historic Preservation. In 1979, it won attention again as it was finally listed in the National Register of Historic Places.

*Above*: Anaconda City Hall with the haunted fire department's engine house located at the rear of the structure. *Library of Congress, item no. mt0123.*

*Right*: Anaconda's city hall incorporated a ninety-foot-tall tower housing a four-sided clock. A twenty-five-foot-tall bell tower was later added to the east end of the building. Both towers have been removed. *Postcard image courtesy of the author.*

The magnificent building was designed by architects Charles Lane and Collins Reber, who won a competition for the best design. They were determined to make the structure as regal as they could while utilizing local labor, Anaconda granite, pressed bricks made locally and even accent trimmings made from Anaconda copper. The final design is considered Romanesque Revival in style, and the building was a beautiful addition to Anaconda's landscape.

Anaconda City Hall was constructed between 1895 and 1896 and cost the city $34,000 in bonds. Jacobson and Company of Anaconda was granted the contract. The original plans incorporated a ninety-foot-tall semi-enclosed tower that housed a four-sided Seth Thomas illuminated clock. A twenty-five-foot-tall bell tower was later added to the east end of the building. It was preferred to use local materials in the construction, such as Anaconda red pressed brick, quarry granite and copper trim and details from Anaconda's very own mines.

In 1901, the building gathered attention when the *Anaconda Standard* commented on its "hauntedness."

## OFFICER POWERS HEARS A GHOST IN 1901

At midnight in early April 1901, a well-respected police officer named William Powers discovered firsthand that the city hall building was haunted.

As he sat at his desk alone in the building one night, a chill ran down his spine. Soon, he heard the unsettling sounds of footsteps. Since a policeman is always on guard, at first, he thought there was an intruder in the building. With his hand on his revolver, he slowly got up from his desk to see who was in the building. Next, he heard a door open. Now, his nerves and senses were on high alert. He drew his weapon. Had a prisoner escaped?

As he walked down the hall to where he heard the noise coming from, he searched everywhere for the phantom trespasser. There was no one anywhere.

The next night, not sure what to think of the strange fiasco, Chief of Police Tom O'Brien offered to stay in the building with Powers to see what would happen. Again, at midnight, both men heard the eerie footsteps. They also heard the front door open (but not close) and other strange noises. Neither of the men ever found a hidden person lurking in the shadows. The bizarre occurrences were never solved but did leave the team disturbed.

One possible ghost "suspect"? An unknown prisoner who was brought in on vagrancy charges, slept for three days straight and then died from alcohol poisoning. Was this prisoner angry that a doctor had not been called, therefore negligently causing his suffering and death?

Over the next few years, many experienced the sounds of doors opening and then ghostly footsteps walking down the hall and continuing on their way. Another possible spooky suspect is a fireman who was rumored to have fallen to his death while coming down the pole.

## ANACONDA'S FEARLESS FIREMEN AND A GHOST

One of the most fascinating and historical true stories of Anaconda comes from very credible witnesses—local firemen.

In 1901, mysterious sounds, heavy phantom footsteps and strange voices were heard during the night in the firehouse. For three nights in a row, fearless fireman Jake Falk was terrorized by disturbing noises he could not make any sense of. Bizarre sounds came from the areas of the firehouse's ladders and headquarters. Sometimes, the noises came from inside the building, and other times, they came from outside. Other firemen on duty began reporting that they heard the frightening sounds as they lay in the cots provided for them. Others reported hearing strange noises near the telephone located at the end of the house.

Falk was touted as one of the bravest men in the department by his captain, Chief Mentrum. Nothing could scare old Falk. And yet he *was* scared.

One night, Falk heard loud sounds coming from the basement. They were so loud that they woke him from a dead sleep. The next night, something strange scared him out of his wits—an eerie sound that came from under his bed.

The next morning, after roll call, the firemen were all chatting about the day's duties when Falk told them of the bizarre noises he had been experiencing in the firehouse. Some men were laughing, and others were intrigued. Together, five of the other firemen decided to volunteer to stay the night with Falk to see if they could figure out what exactly was causing all these weird sounds and calm his nerves.

The men were sitting in the firemen's room, playing cards and whiling away the time, when one man cried out, "I see a face in that window over there!" He yelled and pointed toward the window. He told of a strange apparition he could not explain. The men tried to laugh it off, hoping he was just playing a joke on them.

Next, the crew decided to saunter down to the basement to have a look. The basement led to the county jail. As the men descended the stairs, another fireman yelled out loud and then fell to the ground. He was so startled that he fainted. The men quickly carried him back upstairs and laid him on a bed, hoping he was all right and that his fainting was not caused by a serious health issue. As he regained his composure, he sat up and drank a cup of water. "I saw the same apparition as he saw in the window! It beckoned me to follow it. The ghost sank to the floor as it said this to me."

Falk recalled that he also saw strange apparitions. He told the men, "On Wednesday night, I heard somebody playing a mournful tune on the piano in the sleeping quarters of the fire house. I was all alone."

Who or what was haunting the old firehouse? Firemen are incredible witnesses, as they are not prone to exaggeration or superstition. The men in 1901 were so terrified by the ghosts in their house that they made their statements public through the *Anaconda Standard* on April 11, 1901.

They all firmly believed that the city hall building *was* haunted.

# Deer Lodge Penitentiary

In the 1870s, Deer Lodge Territory was no more violent or lawless than other parts of Montana. The state was not a state yet. Many pioneers and vigilantes took matters into their own hands, stringing criminals up by their necks from any handy hanging tree. Violence escalated.

This prompted the United States government to construct a penitentiary, and it was granted $40,000 to do so. Contractor George McBurney was soon in charge, and the building was completed in 1871. McBurney soon conceived grand plans of constructing a fine hotel in the area as well. He begged and borrowed for any money he could secure for the project.

One of his partners did not feel as confident and soon died by suicide.

The area is considered haunted due to the high number of deaths that occurred there. Almost thirty men died while confined in the prison: five suffered extremely violent deaths, three died by suicide and two more were shot to their early deaths by prison guards. Half of the prisoners were Natives. All the corpses were buried unceremoniously in a small graveyard nearby. The Natives prayed a Great Spirit would take the evil white men by consumption. Later, these bodies were exhumed and moved to another location.

Disturbing a grave is one of the worst ways to unsettle the spirits of the deceased. Many apparitions seen in cemeteries nearby are those of people whose bodies were dislocated; they either seek revenge or remain unsettled for some reason. There are thousands of hidden or unmarked graves throughout the world. Often, pioneers and cowboys would just bury their dead where they were shot or dropped dead. Along the Oregon Trail, the pioneers had no choice but to leave the bodies of their loved ones behind as they pushed onward, burying them in hastily dug graves with makeshift tombstones. Today, there are countless homes and buildings that were built right on top of the dead without anyone knowing—that is, until a ghosts appears.

The area and grounds where this prison once stood could harbor the angry spirits of the men who died violently at the hands of each other and the guards.

# ANACONDA'S BABY GRAVEYARD

An urban legend that began sometime around the 1970s is still being told around campfires today. There is a bizarre site in Anaconda near a hill where

The symbol of a lamb on a gravestone signifies that the buried individual is a baby or infant. *Library of Congress, item no. afc1981005_82415; Paula J. Johnson, photographer.*

many babies were supposedly buried in unmarked graves. Who were these babies? The legend says that if you drive over to the hill and put your automobile in neutral, the car will mysteriously move up toward the hill.

Some people have sprinkled baby powder on their car's trunks or hoods, only to later find the tiny handprints of a baby pressed into the powder.

Is there any truth to this legend? Where does Anaconda's baby graveyard exist?

It remains a mystery.

# MYSTERIOUS LIGHTS OVER ANACONDA'S SMOKESTACK

The 585-foot-tall smelter stack in Anaconda can be seen from I-90, signaling your approach to the town. The structure measures 75 feet across at the base and 60 feet across at the top. It is the tallest surviving masonry structure in the world.

The stack was built in 1918 as part of the Washoe Smelter of the Anaconda Copper Mining Company, owned by Marcus Daly. While it was in operation, it was designed to carry hot exhaust gases up and out of the

The smokestack was the largest and tallest man-made structure at the time, measuring 585 feet tall and 86 feet wide at the base. The walls were 5.5 feet thick. *Postcard image courtesy of the author.*

main flue that carried gases from various roasting and smelting furnaces. The stack is located half a mile up a hill from the original smelter. The stack was constructed of 2,464,652 locally made bricks. The builders were from Alphons Custodis Chimney Construction of New York.

The old Washoe Smelter was demolished in 1981, but the stack was saved by local citizens. In 1986, it became the Anaconda Smokestack State Park.

Mysterious flashing lights have been seen hovering over the smokestack by many witnesses over the years. No one knows who or what is causing these unexplained lights. Are they UFOs? Are they supernatural orbs from unearthly entities?

*Note: Once, while the author herself was staying at Gunslinger Gulch, she witnessed these strange lights along with about ten other visitors. Although all of the witnesses tried to capture a photograph of the mysterious lights, no one could get a clear picture. Why was it impossible to capture the lights, even with professional equipment?*

# 4

# Ghost Towns and Terrors

## Anaconda's Very Haunted (and Almost Famous) Gunslinger Gulch Guest Ranch

*We're seeing people* [ghosts] *more often. We're feeling things more often. It starts off with a touch; next thing you know, it could be a scratch. Things are getting weirder.*
—*Cameron, the son of Karen Broussard, the ranch owner*

The eerie, real-life ghost town called Gunslinger Gulch is nestled on the outskirts of Anaconda proper. It is so haunted that after many paranormal investigators researched the parcel, they *all* determined that multiple spirits roam the grounds and buildings. The ghost town caught so much attention that it soon was being investigated for the Discovery Channel's series called *Ghost Town Terror*.

A paranormal research team, Tim Wood and Sapphire Sandalo, spent several weeks trying to discover (and hopefully move toward the light) any mischievous spirits that were plaguing the town and causing distress to Karen Broussard and her family, her daughter Chloe and sons Cameron and Colby.

The property is unique; it is made up of a collection of nineteen buildings that were each rescued or salvaged from Anaconda or nearby towns. These buildings are situated on fifty-two picturesque acres. The full history of

The saloon and brothel at Gunslinger Gulch in the summer. Spirits do not seem to care what the weather is and continue to haunt the buildings regardless of the snow or heat. *Courtesy of the author.*

each building is unknown, as it was not formally documented, but the few buildings that are known about have creepy links that can be validated by facts and verified as such.

The ghost town was developed by its former owner Sherri Jamison and was called the 1880s Ranch. The tiny town on Cable Road sat vacant for a time and then went up for sale.

> *The original owner had salvaged all these buildings from demo in local communities in and around Anaconda and then hauled them all out here to build this.*
> *—Karen Broussard, the current owner of Gunslinger Gulch*

This is where the current owner and her family stepped in, during the late winter of 2019. Karen Broussard was living in the Seattle area when she spotted the property listed for sale. Curious about the ghost town and desperately wanting out of Seattle, she made an offer on the ranch. Low and behold, she was now the proud owner of a bizarre property in

Anaconda, Montana. Her house sold quickly, and soon, she and her older children were making the six-hundred-mile trip to a town they had never even been to before.

Once there, they discovered the property needed major work. Plumbing and water issues abounded. Electrical issues needed to be repaired. Cleanup, painting, yard work—it seemed to never end. But the Broussard family was determined to make this happen, so they all rolled up their sleeves and dug in. After several long months, the "town" was finally coming together.

A new name for the property was needed, and the brand Gunslinger Gulch was adopted. It is appropriately called a gulch, because the acreage is nestled between Levengood Gulch and English Gulch.

Gunslinger Gulch comprises nineteen various buildings, the notorious ones being a church, a saloon, a brothel, a white boardinghouse, a bathhouse, a round cordwood cabin, a two-cell jailhouse, a sod house, a slab house, an old laundry building, a log cabin and a traveler wagon. Although no documents can be found, some say that both of the saloon/brothel combination buildings came from the east end of Anaconda, down by the smelter factory. The church was moved to its current location from a ranch in nearby Philipsburg. The former owner Sherri knew of one ghost that haunted the buildings for sure, although she herself is a skeptic. The other buildings were brought over from the nearby towns of Deer Lodge and Racetrack.

## The Jail

*In the jailhouse, there is a spirit who is protective of the area and will make themselves known only to people who are pushing it or trying to say there is nothing there. It can be something as small as a breath, but also, a guest was touched and ran out of the bathroom from it.*
—Benjamin Young, Cross Country Paranormal

Surprisingly, the old jailhouse is the least active building in the gulch, but it still carries a ghost or two.

The other buildings are another story.

Buildings often carry residual energy that can somehow be "trapped" within the walls, especially if it was the place of a negative or traumatic event, such as a murder or death by suicide. Even with special ghost hunting equipment, it is unclear who (or what) is haunting Gunslinger Gulch. Multiple

The jailhouse at Gunslinger Gulch appears to be the least haunted building there, although many claim this is the building where visitors are most often "touched" by a spirit. *Courtesy of the author.*

paranormal teams have stayed at the ranch in the hopes of capturing clear and undeniable proof of the unearthly activities that abound there. Psychic mediums have also come to the gulch to see if they can determine the cause of the activity and sightings. Many tourists and guests have experienced the unexplained while staying at the bed-and-breakfast.

## The Log Cabin

*When I was in the log cabin…I heard loud footsteps from outside the door. Then the doorknob turned, and the door swung open at full force. It was really scary. It really shook me in my boots!*
—Chloe Broussard, the daughter of Karen Broussard

*The log cabin* [has] *the heaviest feeling. There is a male figure in there who is very protective of the back room and will do its best to scare people out of the cabin. It likes to appear on the ceiling and above the*

61

*bathroom to make himself seem bigger and looking down on you. We
have captured him on the SLS camera and actually confined him to the
bed with iron spikes. We have a video of the bathroom door opening on
its own and of a dark mass lunging off the bed at us.*
—Benjamin Young, Cross Country Paranormal

*There's somebody* [a spirit] *in that back room.
They're not happy. They're not friendly.*
—Karen Broussard, owner

The log cabin rental seems to hold the most paranormal activity in the gulch. Although no records indicate where the building originally came from, most of the gulch's buildings were built in the late 1800s and early 1900s. Some suggest a man hanged himself in the building a long time ago and that his restless ghost still lingers in the back bedroom. The sturdy rafters could certainly hold the weight of a man if one wished to die by suicide by hanging from them.

A man's raspy voice is often heard coming from the back bedroom, along with the sounds of his laughter. Does he enjoy scaring people? Why is he laughing?

Some who visit the log cabin experience an overwhelming sense of sadness and feel like crying for no reason.

If the ghost is not a man who hanged himself, then there might be another spirit who is haunting the cabin. It is recorded that one of the small buildings was brought to Anaconda from a very small town called Racetrack.

Racetrack is located just twelve miles from Anaconda. It acquired its name because the local Natives would race their ponies through the open pastures. Some of the earliest documented horse races were run in Racetrack. A successful Deer Lodge banker named S.E. Larabie raced his beautiful Thoroughbred horses in town. He kept his prized horses at a stable called the Willow Brook Race Farm near Deer Lodge in the 1880s. The town of Racetrack is very small, comprising less than one square mile. It has never been a large town. In 2020, the population was counted at just forty-two. A town of one square mile cannot hold very many buildings.

With illegal gambling, excessive drinking, betting on horses and violence abounding over the race results, many attacks and even murders occurred there. If a man put all his money on a horse and lost, the outcome could bankrupt him within seconds. And other gamblers did not take well to *not* paying off any debts. They would just as soon

The log cabin is the most haunted building at Gunslinger Gulch. Many feel the overwhelming desire to cry when they are in it, and others feel a male entity bullying them. *Courtesy of the author.*

kill those who owed them—and many times did. No one knows which building was brought over to Gunslinger Gulch from Racetrack, but it is fairly obvious that it might still hold residual energy from a bet gone wrong that resulted in a murder. Any tragedy can trap negative energy inside a structure, even if that structure is moved to another location. Does one of the small cabins or houses at the ranch hold the spirit of a gambler who died at Racetrack?

The mystery of who exactly is haunting the log cabin in Gunslinger Gulch may never be solved.

*Note: The author has stayed in the log cabin personally, along with her sister Sue, and they both can testify to hearing a disembodied male voice as well as the sounds of heavy footsteps and male laughter. Neither the author nor her sister was able to sleep in the bedroom in the back of the building; instead, they ended up bunking together in the front room and remained awake most of the night. The noises they heard included a male coughing, and they smelled cigarette or cigar smoke (when nobody was smoking).*

## *The Church*

The old, beautiful church where the Broussard family lives has a more sinister ghost within its walls. The church was originally moved to the gulch from a ranch in the nearby small town of Phillipsburg. The peeling paint and cracked boards have seen better days, but the looming presence of the majestic building is amazing. A homemade cross is secured at the very top of the towering steeple.

The church emerges into view as guests drive up the main road of Gunslinger Gulch. Surrounded by beautiful horses, goats, chickens and geese, the serene image of a peaceful home doesn't seem far off.

But inside the church hides a more sinister visitor: a male entity that has attached itself to Karen. When Tim, Sapphire and Sarah calmly try to get the spirit to communicate and tell them *why* he is haunting the building, they are slammed with a loud "GET OUT! GO!" EVP instead.

Inside its walls something hidden and dark is lurking in the shadows. A male apparition lingers in the corner. Karen was put into a trance state and

The beautiful but haunted old church at Gunslinger Gulch, where Karen Broussard and her family live with an angry entity. *Courtesy of the author.*

when asked who is haunting her, she tried to reply, "Orniasi" or "Ornasis." She stumbled on the word. Basically, she was trying to describe a dark shadow figure that is a shape shifter and can also be considered a vampire demon. The correct term is *Ornias*, a strange demonic entity that can sometimes prey on the living and drive them to the point of madness.

But who is the dark figure that lingers unwanted within the walls of the beautiful church? It is revealed that possibly the ghost is a man from the family's past who was killed in a tragic accident. If that is so, why would he be wanting to scare the family? What does he seek?

The answers are unclear, as in many hauntings.

## The Saloon

*In the bar/kitchen area, there is a tall shadow figure that is seen pacing near the back bathroom. As Karen and myself were speaking, we both saw him out of the corner of our eye. Based on the size and shape of the shadow, it was a male figure but nonthreatening.*
—*Benjamin Young, Cross Country Paranormal*

The saloon and dining area and the brothel at Gunslinger Gulch are actually two buildings that were connected once they were moved to the current parcel. Paranormal investigators have discovered a connection between one of the haunted buildings and the famous Dumas Brothel that is located in nearby Butte, Montana. The other building (now the saloon) was formerly owned by John and Katherine Harrington (both of Irish descent) in the early 1900s. They lived there together. Years later, their granddaughter Marie Theresa (Harrington) Evans was brutally murdered at the Empire Hotel in Butte in 1940. (Note: See the section titled "Theresa Evans's Murder and a Haunted Saloon.")

Although the police had several suspects, her killer (or killers) was never captured. The coroner performed an autopsy and ruled her death a homicide. The cause of death was "subdural hemorrhage over the right cerebral hemisphere causing pressure on the brain due to external violence at the hands of a person or persons unknown." Her jaw was broken, she had been choked and some of her teeth had even been pushed down into her throat.

Does Theresa haunt her old family home that is now part of Gunslinger Gulch? Is her spirit residing there because it connects with happier times,

The haunted bar in the saloon section of Gunslinger Gulch, where many claim to see both a *cat-sith* (black cat) apparition, as well as several other ghosts. *Courtesy of the author.*

prior to her murder? If her grandmother offered her and her sister security and safety in that home, it would only make sense that Theresa's restless spirit still seeks refuge there.

## Theresa Evans's Murder and a Haunted Saloon

*They never found her* [Theresa's] *killer,*
*and that restless energy can create a haunting.*
—*Tim Wood, paranormal investigator*

One of the most bizarre, almost forgotten and unsolved vicious murders that occurred in the area was that of an Anaconda woman named Theresa Evans (1902–1940). Although she was killed on April 18, 1940, in room no. 9 at the Empire Hotel, located at 101 South Wyoming Street in nearby Butte, her history and livelihood remained in Anaconda.

It was later learned that Theresa was the granddaughter of the Harringtons, who formerly owned the saloon that was later moved to become part of Gunslinger Gulch.

66

Another possible explanation for the hauntings of the buildings is that two of the structures were moved to Gunslinger Gulch from the east end of the city by the factory and smelter, where Theresa's husband once worked. He was a suspect in her murder and possibly continues to haunt the buildings for unknown reasons.

Theresa had a rough go in life, and nothing ever seemed to turn out right for her. Although she was hardworking and kind, her decisions regarding men were not the best. She was married four times, and all of the marriages failed. She worked as a waitress at both the lucrative Montana Hotel Bar, located at 200 Main Street Southwest, and the Owl Saloon, located at 819 East Third Street in Anaconda (when it was still called Goosetown). She had five kids. The youngest two were always in tow but were raised by their grandmother, Theresa's mom, Mary Greene, in Anaconda.

Theresa soon found herself in love with a man named Nick, and they were married in 1938. He would later be her possible killer.

Despite her mother's warnings of marrying a man she barely knew, Theresa married Nick anyway in the hopes of establishing a new and better life for herself and her two youngest children, Jeanne and Raymond. Nick

The saloon and dining building of Gunslinger Gulch with the brothel portion upstairs. Many have felt the warm touch of a woman and a menacing threat from a man in the brothel. *Courtesy of the author.*

An unidentified patron (possibly proprietor Richmond Miller) tending the bar at the Hotel Montana. In 1902, rooms cost $3.50 a day. The hotel was closed in 1976. *Library of Congress, item no. 100235p.*

worked at the smelter in Anaconda and also wanted a better life, away from the smoke and pollution caused by the Anaconda Copper Company. He caught wind that the Belmont Bar in Butte was up for sale and quickly convinced Theresa that this could be the break they were both needing.

Leaving the children in the care of their grandmother, Theresa and Nick moved to Butte to start their new adventure together.

They decided to risk what little they had to purchase the Belmont Bar on South Arizona Street, securing funding from a dangerous local loan shark and hustler named Milo Ivankovich.

Everything started out positive but soon took a nosedive for the worse. It seemed that no matter how long and hard they worked, they could not turn a profit. Nick reassured Theresa each month that next month would be better if they just worked harder. Theresa blindly trusted Nick, which was her first mistake in the tumultuous relationship.

But soon, the long hours, lack of profit and constant fighting took a toll on their marriage. Unknown to Theresa, Nick had a gambling problem and had been using their profits in poker games. The Belmont Bar soon fell behind in payments to Ivankovich, who was not pleased. *Nobody* ever cheated him out of a single penny.

A gangster was sent to follow Nick and Theresa to give them a very stern warning that they better pay off their debt—or there would be hell to pay.

Nick quietly disappeared, leaving Theresa to run the Belmont alone, which was impossible to do. She just could not believe that Nick would leave her and their dreams high and dry. Months went by, and there was still no sign of Nick or their past profits.

Ivankovich sent a thug named Cabby Young to trail Teresa and hopefully get his money. Yet Theresa took a liking to Young, and soon, they were close friends. Theresa was a pretty and fun woman—he could do worse. Although Young reported back to Ivankovich that he firmly believed Terresa had no idea (nor cared) where Nick had disappeared to, Ivankovich still wanted his money back, no matter what it took.

After disappearing for several months, Nick eventually found his way back to Butte, searching for Theresa in disguise. When he saw her flirting with Young, he went mad with jealousy. Theresa had just rented her own room at the Empire, so she no longer had to share with a roommate. This gave her the utmost privacy if she desired to entertain a male guest.

There were several people who may have wanted Theresa dead for various reasons:

- Ivankovich was furious at Nick and Theresa for never repaying their loan. Since they could never find Nick, it was suspected the men could have taken their anger out on poor Theresa.
- Nick, Theresa's fourth husband, became infuriated that Theresa had a new love in her life. Jealousy is a very good motive for murder.
- A female friend of Nick's named "Mickey" (formerly Michelle) McCarthy was pretending to be a man so she could secure work in town. When Theresa discovered that she was actually a girl, she threatened Mickey's livelihood. Would that be a reason to murder Theresa—to keep her mouth shut?
- Was it Cabby Young, her new beau, who killed her? Was he really a mad man or violent predator?
- Or was her killer a complete stranger, and Theresa was just in the wrong place at the wrong time?

The staircase in the Empire Hotel, which served as lodgings for prostitutes. Theresa Evans's killer descended these very stairs after beating her to a pulp. *Library of Congress, item no. 101104p.*

Yet on this particular night in April, the killer would finally have his (or her) chance to kill Theresa. She was alone in room no. 9, eagerly waiting for her new lover, Cabby Young, to enter her apartment to make love to her. Whether their lovemaking ever happened is still a mystery.

Marian Grant lived across the hall in the Empire in room no. 6. Theresa and Marian had only known each other for a few weeks, but they had become fast friends.

At 7:00 a.m. on April 19, Marian was passing Theresa's room when she noticed her door was slightly ajar. She called for Theresa but soon heard strange moaning and cries. When she entered room no. 9, she was aghast to see her new friend lying in a pool of blood, her face and upper torso badly beaten—almost unrecognizable. The sheriff's officers quickly took Theresa to the county hospital.

But at the hospital, Theresa's outlook did not look good. She had suffered a severe blow to her head that resulted in brain damage, and the doctors agreed she would not survive. She never regained consciousness, and her cerebral hemorrhaging got worse.

Theresa was soon dead. Unfortunately, she was never able to reveal her killer (or killers) to the police.

Whatever happened that fatal night—or early morning—remains a tragic and disturbing mystery. Theresa's murder was never solved, her killer never captured or punished. Theresa Evans would never get justice for her horrible murder.

Theresa was the daughter of Frederick and Mary Greene, both pioneer residents of Anaconda. She attended St. Paul Parochial School and then Anaconda High School. After Coroner Con Sheehy performed his autopsy, Theresa's battered body was moved to the Lavish Merrill Mortuary in Anaconda, later to be taken home to the Greene residence at 607 East City Street in town.

She was buried at Mt. Olivet Cemetery in Anaconda.

Some believe her restless spirit still haunts the old location of the Empire Hotel. Others feel her ghost returned to Anaconda, where she and her children once lived happily together. Others think her ghost hangs out in the

The Copper block was built by the Nadeau Investment Company in 1892. Later, as the Empire Hotel, the site of Theresa Evans's brutal, unsolved murder in 1940. *Library of Congress, item no. 101103p.*

Montana Hotel in Anaconda, where she once worked, still trying to make enough money to pay off the Belmont Bar debt she owed Ivankovich, even in the afterlife.

*Note: For the full story of Theresa Evans's life and mysterious murder, please read* Lady in Room Number Nine *by Larry Ohman. Theresa was his grandmother, and his research on Theresa's life and untimely death is both fascinating and well-written.*

## The Dumas Brothel

Theresa Evans (whose ghost haunts the saloon and brothel at Gunslinger Gulch) was also said to work at the Dumas Brothel in Butte as a prostitute once she fell on hard times after her husband stole their savings and left her. She started living at the Empire Hotel, just one block away from the Dumas, in the red-light district. It was rumored that sex workers would go to the Empire for drinks after their shift at the Dumas. If Theresa Evans lived (and was murdered) at the Empire Hotel but also worked at the Dumas, a connection between the two buildings could have been formed.

Also, if it was true that she was working as a sex worker at the Dumas, it seems likely that she would also feel comfortable in the brothel back at Gunslinger Gulch (the building that was once her family's own residence). Is Theresa's spirit one of the entities that is haunting both the Dumas and Gunslinger's brothel?

The Dumas Brothel is still standing today at 45 East Mercury Street. It operated as a busy prostitution house between 1890 and 1982, when its doors and dirty cribs were finally closed for good (for tax evasion). Although the actual connection between the Dumas Brothel in Butte and the brothel and saloon buildings at Gunslinger Gulch has yet to be fully discovered, one thing is certain: several naughty spirits have clung to the buildings and continue to taunt guests at the gulch to this day. Some tell of a warm hand touching them (sometimes inappropriately), as if inviting them to join them in a night of passion and fun. Others have felt the soft caress across their face or shoulder, as if giving comfort.

Perhaps the history of the Dumas might bring to light a connection?

Dumas is located in the heart of what was known as the Venus District, a crime-ridden red-light section of town. The ghost of a woman has been seen walking up and down the stairs, sometimes carrying a suitcase. Is this the same ghost that haunted the gulch's brothel?

The Dumas was opened in 1890 by two brothers, Arthur and Joseph Nadeau, who came to Montana from Canada. Joseph also owned the Windsor Hotel in town on Broadway. They sold their intertest in the Dumas in 1900 to Grace McGinnis. When she took over, there were just four ladies of ill fame working there, and they charged fifty cents per deed.

In the 1920s through the mid-1930s, Madame Gertrude "Gertie" Pikanen ran the Dumas. She was a slave driver and forced the sex workers to service as many as fifty men each per day. She also had a more sinister side to her; Gertie was known to perform and force illegal abortions on her working girls. If the girls refused and carried their babies to full term, Gertie would lie and tell the mother that the baby had died, when in reality, she would snatch them from their mothers and sell them to strangers for $500. Sadly, she was rumored to have sold fourteen babies. The whereabouts and futures of these babies will never be known.

Paranormal researchers and visitors to the Dumas Brothel report feeling like they were punched in the stomach and having severe pain in their abdominal areas. Could these strange occurrences somehow be linked to the illegal abortions Gertie inflicted on her girls and the pain they must have felt?

In the 1940s, the madam of the Dumas was a woman named Lillian Walden, who ran the brothel until 1950. The United States government tried in vain to close the Dumas and surrounding brothels so that the spread of diseases would not affect the soldiers who were going to war.

When the Dumas was running smoothly, the upper floor was used by rich patrons and was serviced by upper-class call girls. The basement was for the down-on-their luck men and dirty, poor workers, and it was appropriately serviced by common or lower-class working girls.

There was a private passageway that led from the Dumas to Venus Alley, Pleasant Alley and, eventually, Piss Alley. These alleys were lined with cramped and flea-bitten cribs where the lowest working girls worked. Nightly shootings, stabbings, robberies and beatings were common there. The basement was eventually sealed off.

From 1950 to 1955, the madam of the Dumas was Elinor Knott (1912–1955). Knott was originally from Colorado. Her death remains unsolved. Some think hers may be the spirit that continues to haunt both locations. Elinor desperatly wanted to leave the brothel business behind her and start a new life. She fell in love with a married man from Butte, and in February 1955, they decided to run away together. The lovestruck Elinor eagerly packed her suitcase, ready for the next phase of her life to begin. But that day never came. Her lover never showed up.

Elinor Knott was heartbroken and angry at the age of forty two; it is uncertain what really happened on that long and fateful night.

The next day, Elinor's dead body was found in the upstairs madam's room no. 20 by a sex worker named Bonita Farren. It was reported that Elinor died from a cerebral hemorrhage. Others claim she took her own life out of sadness and desperation by a lethal overdose of pills and alcohol.

The one person to benefit from her death? The next in line to become the madam of the house, Bonita. She quickly took over the business and also took over ownership of Elinor's red Cadillac convertible and Harley Davidson motorcycle. She also began wearing Elinor's private jewelry, the collection of which was extensive.

Knott's ghostly figure has been seen in every room of the Dumas.

Suspiciously, Farren's husband, John, died tragically. He supposedly fell down a flight of stairs in the back of the Dumas. John had worked at a saloon called the Board of Trade in Butte. Did the ruthless Bonita push him down the stairs? His death also remains a mystery. Perhaps John's restless and angry spirit still lingers at the base of the stairs, where his once bloody corpse lay.

A woman named Ruby Garrett (also known as Lee Arrigoni) came to Butte and took over the ownership of the Dumas in 1941. At that time, the women who were working in the lower cribs were charged $2.50 in rent per day and took home less than 40 percent of their profits.

Ruby had an abusive and uncaring husband. One night in 1959, while he was involved in a poker game, Ruby waltzed into the room and coolly shot him in cold blood. She spent just nine months in jail for manslaughter and then resumed running the Dumas. It is interesting to note that Bonita's husband, John, was working at the bar the night Ruby shot and killed her husband.

Things ran smoothly until twenty-two years later, in 1981, the IRS got wind that Ruby was evading paying her taxes. During this time, the girls were being paid only $20 for each client. The $21,539 Ruby owed in back taxes earned her another stint in jail at the California State Penitentiary, this time for six months.

The Dumas finally closed its doors as a brothel for good in 1982. Today, it is being restored to be used as a museum, and the current owner thinks he is also somehow linked to the past of the notorious Dumas Brothel.

*Note: The Dumas Brothel was also featured on an episode of* The Dead Files *in 2011 (season 8, episode 1).*

# *The* Cat-sith

*I've seen apparitions. I've heard voices coming from rooms. I was
alone in the saloon and saw what was a cat. It leapt off the bar and
disappeared before it hit the ground. When I crawled underneath the
building, I found a mummified cat skeleton.*
—Cameron Broussard, Karen Broussard's son

The brothel accommodations and the saloon downstairs at Gunslinger
house multiple ghosts and even a phantom cat.

The cat ghost began showing up right after Karen and her family moved in.
Although they had no cats and did not see a stray anywhere, they continued
to hear the soft meowing (and sometimes hissing) of a feline. Night after
night, they tried to find the phantom cat but to no avail. They would feel the
cat jump up onto their bed, but when they looked, no cat was there.

Later, when a worker and Cameron had to go under the saloon floor for
repairs, they found the skeleton of a black cat underneath the building.

Today, the ghost cat's skeleton is displayed by the bar.

Some still claim they can hear ghostly meowing and the occasional hissing
seemingly from thin air. Do animals have spirits that can choose to haunt in
the afterlife? Many say yes.

The Harringtons were Irish, and in Irish folklore, a black cat's ghost is
called a *cat-sith*. The legend of the cat-sith warns that it is a fairy creature
that can shapeshift into the form of a black cat and has the capability to
steal the soul of the unburied. During a funeral, it is said that no fires can
be lit near the body, as cat-sith are attracted to their warmth. The saloon at
Gunslinger Gulch has a large wood stove in it that Karen sits in front of for
hours for comfort. Does the cat-sith curl up next to her in order to comfort
her or to try to steal her soul? By keeping the mummified cat carcass on the
property, are the Broussards promoting the cat-sith to remain in the saloon?

Black cats have gotten a bad rap and have had a negative connotation as
far back as the dark ages. During this era, the black cat was associated with
witches, and they were classified as the personal favorite animal of the devil.
During the Salem witch trials, any black cats that were seen in the area were
captured and killed along with any witches. Where did the black cat come
from at Gunslinger Gulch? Does it really haunt the buildings? Dozens of
people have seen or heard Gunslinger's ghost cat, and many find comfort in
its presence—others are terrified.

When Tim and Sapphire made an EVP recording in the saloon, they heard the words "Get help."

Local medium Sarah Lemos visited the saloon building with Karen, Tim, Sapphire and Cameron. They all immediately felt freezing cold spots and heard strange paranormal voices. Their equipment also began recording strange phenomenon. Lemos told Karen, "They know you. Have you ever felt someone come up behind you?" After a brief pause, Karen responded, "Yes, I've had somebody come up behind me and put both hands on my shoulders."

Who is touching visitors and the Broussard family? Although the ghosts do not seem to be physically harmful, the experience of being touched by icy, unseen hands can quite startling.

## *The Brothel above the Saloon*

*There's this one window over on the back side, I don't know how many times I'd close that window and yet it'd be open. I mean open.*
—Pat Scalise, a previous caretaker of the ranch

The brothel unit is located above the saloon, and as one makes their way up the steep and narrow steps to the second story, you can almost *feel* a time change. Once upstairs, guests are greeted by old-style wallpaper, ornate cast-iron beds and lamps from days gone by.

The very air seems to change.

It is easy to visualize working women plying their trade in such a room that was built for pleasure.

But what paranormal investigators Tim and Sapphire, along with psychic medium Sarah Lemos, felt was anything but pleasure when they spent time in the brothel.

Objects moved on their own, flashlights turned on and off to answer questions, faint odors of both cigarette smoke and perfume drifted by and a window opened over and over again (even though it was latched) in the brothel unit. Some guests have said they saw the apparition of a man looming over the bed. Others claim to have seen a woman smoking a cigarette, staring out the window at the street below. Could this possibly be the ghost of a sex worker and one of her customers?

## The Boardinghouse

*In the boardinghouse, we often hear a woman's voice calling, "Hello!"*
*—Karen Broussard, owner*

*When I was visiting Gunslinger Gulch, my friend and I went into the*
*boardinghouse alone one night. We slowly walked up the stairs that*
*led to the bedroom on the second floor. We only had a small flashlight*
*with us. We put the flashlight down on the corner of the handrail and*
*then sat down on the bed together, waiting. We asked the ghosts several*
*questions. All of a sudden, the flashlight clicked off and also bent itself*
*back to the "closed" position! When I got up to turn the flashlight back*
*on (and open it back up), I discovered how hard it was to reopen it.*
*There is no way it could have done that by itself. Obviously, an entity*
*performed this action to let us know it was there!*
*—Deborah Cuyle, the author, from her last visit to Gunslinger Gulch*

The boardinghouse has multiple ghosts residing in it. Some people (this author included) have seen a pair of small children at the top of the stairs. Others see a woman's figure. People have also reported seeing dark shadow figures in the corner of the upstairs bedroom. Objects moving is also common.

The boardinghouse at Gunslinger Gulch carries two small child entities as well as a female ghost that often says, "Hello!" *Courtesy of the author.*

Was the boardinghouse once a schoolhouse? Since there are no records of the original building or its previous use, it is hard to say. Are the two small ghostly figures those of twins who once resided in the house when it was a private residence? Again, it is hard to say.

## The Cordwood House

*I was in bed, and I heard this voice right over by the window,*
*looking over me, but there was nobody there, absolutely nothing.*
*It felt like it had a hold over me, like I couldn't defy against it.*
*I felt I was being paralyzed.*
*—Colby Broussard, Karen Broussard's son*

*In the portal house, there are a number of spirits I believe to be passing*
*through. I don't think there is just one who stays there;*
*I believe that house is the one that the spirts of the property come*
*through and leave through if they decide to leave. In there, we had*
*a number of spirits coming through the portal device, and one guest*
*reported a burning on their back, and when we looked,*
*there were faint scratch marks on their back.*
*—Cross Country Paranormal*

The cordwood house is a beautiful and complex unit that was constructed from round cords of wood and some sort of cement mixture. It has glass bottles mixed here and there into the round walls, which emit a gorgeous kaleidoscope of various colors that bounce off the walls inside the room. The roof is held up by a gigantic chunk of vertical lumber with many thick logs, each propped on top of the main perpendicular log to form the round roof. The building itself is quite a masterpiece of unique architecture. It has an open concept with two beds with a nice bathroom.

Some guests claim they saw a mysterious figure lurking in the shadows outside the cordwood house. Others are terrified when they discover a ghost peering in a window. Faint scratches are often found on a person's body after they stay the night in the house. Who is peering in through the windows when no one is outside?

Although there seems to be several entities hanging around the cordwood building, who they are or why they remain has not been revealed yet.

## The Demonic Hole on the Property

*If I could imagine where a dark energy would be, this would be it.*
*I can only imagine what's at the bottom of it. It's not a place for the*
*living; it is a place for the dead.*
*—Tim Wood*

The deep, creepy hole situated away from the ranch but within the parcel's fifty-two acres has a menacing and very frightening presence. Why is it there? Is it man-made or a natural phenomenon? Is it a sinkhole or something else? How long has it been there? How deep is it? Are there skeletal remains of murder victims nestled deep down where no one can ever find them?

The hole presents more secrets and questions than any definitive answers.

When a rock is thrown into the hole, the final, resounding *clank* as it hits the bottom is never heard.

Sinkholes naturally occur all over the world. They are created when water erodes underlying dirt and rock, creating a unique opening. When it rains, the water has nowhere to drain, so it fills up and then slowly leaks back to the subsurface.

But the hole at Gunslinger Gulch appears to be something else. Did some long-forgotten miner slowly dig the hole by hand in search of his fortune in buried copper? Anaconda is famous for its stash of copper ore. Many men were made wealthy from the contents discovered inside the mountains.

An EVP that was recorded in the hole captured an unknown entity saying, "Come on down here." Later, the paranormal investigators thought the ghost was telling them to go back to the saloon, not down into the hole. The crew was able to see bones in the hole. Where did the bones come from? Are they animal or human bones? Did a deer or some other animal fall into the hole, become trapped and die?

Someday, a camera or drone may be lowered into the hole to find out what is really down there, lurking in the total darkness. Until then, the hole remains just one more mystery at Gunslinger Gulch.

## The House on Commercial Avenue

*When we first moved to Anaconda, I drove past this house,*
*and it literally captured my heart. When I look at it,*
*somehow I feel it saying, "Welcome home."*
*—Karen Broussard, the owner of Gunslinger Gulch*

Karen Broussard feels a very strong connection to a house she spotted when she and her children moved to Anaconda. Although she seldom leaves Gunslinger Gulch, when she does, she finds herself driving by an old, vacant house at 402 East Commercial Avenue. The house is a local curiosity, and many people are fascinated by it. The two-story home does have a sense of intrigue about it, even though many claim it is haunted.

*Note: The history of the home has been fairly elusive and is revealed now by the author in this chapter. Many of the facts are hard to find, and many dates and names conflict (which is common for older homes), but much like a puzzle, the picture emerges. Since there seems to be such great interest in the history of this home, the author has tried to create its history as accurately as possible. Please forgive any mistakes made!*

The lovely home was once the private residence of Dennis Shovlin (1843–1926) and his wife, Lucy (1857–1938). Dennis was originally from Ardara, Donegal, Ireland. He immigrated to America in 1857, when he was just fourteen years old. Lucy Davis was born in Indiana. They were married in 1885 in Indiana. Dennis apparently adopted Lucy's son, Edgar B. Dockter, who was born on September 12, 1882, the son of Samuel Dockter. The family moved to Anaconda, Montana, around 1890. Dennis ran for mayor of Anaconda in 1891. The city took note, as Dennis was not only a house painter but one of the town's very first interior decorators as well.

In 1888, the building on that particular Commercial Avenue lot was different, along with the address and street name. The road was called First Street (now Commercial Avenue), the structure was a one-story home (not two) and the address was 404 not 402. There was also a smaller cabin on the property. In 1891, the map shows a Chinese laundry and tenant lodgings on the parcel.

In 1896, the Sanborn map for that parcel reveals no structure, so the orginal structure was either torn down or burned down. It is logical that the Shovlins rented a home until they built their residence on the property. In 1897, a new building was recorded on the Sanborn map; it was used as a hotel, and the census shows it had multiple boarders.

In 1900, Dennis; his wife, Lucy; their son, Edgar; and a boarder named William Powers (a policeman by trade) lived on the property.

In April 1901, Edgar saw his first ghost. He was walking home past the old city hall and fire station around midnight when he remembered his friend Fireman Groatty was working the midnight shift. He stopped by and was going to say hello. Groatty was asleep on the floor. When the two men went

The once-beautiful mansion at 402 East Commercial Avenue. Although it has a checkered past, it also created many loving memories for many people. Karen Broussard from Gunslinger Gulch feels drawn to the home for unexplained reasons. *Courtesy of Google Earth.*

to open the door, they both saw the apparition of a man. Both men were scared to death. Edgar ran all the way home.

In 1903, a grand, new structure appeared on the Sanborn map, the outline clearly showing the home that still stands there today and still carries the 404 address. The building to the right of the Shovlin home was a hand laundry. In 1904, the home was elaborately decorated with pink and white flowers and decorations for Dennis's niece Julia Marshall and her groom John Casey in order to host an elegant wedding. The entire town was in awe at its beauty.

The Shovlin family lived happily in the home for many years. Dennis Shovlin worked as a street commissioner for several years and was praised for using crushed rock materials to replace the wooden planks in the construction of the streets of Anaconda. In 1909, he pushed for the luxury of using cement for streets and sidewalks. He also became a member of Montana's legislature. In 1910, the Shovlin home had many boarders (most house painters like Dennis), possibly to earn the family extra money. During the 1920s, the home was known for hosting fun and fancy Halloween parties. Edgar enjoyed dancing and entertaining, even though he worked as a boiler maker. In 1901, Edgar accidentally fell under a streetcar and was run over. Due to this accident, all of his toes were sliced off, and eventually, his entire foot had to be amputated. As a dancer, this mutilation was personally devastating and severely depressing. (He also had a small stroke in 1910.)

But on June 5, 1926, the fun came to end, as Dennis tragically died of a heart attack in the home at the age of eighty-two. His funeral was held in the parlor of the family home two days later. His widow, Lucy, and son, Edgar, were overcome by grief. But Lucy and her son tried to continue with their lives.

Yet another tragedy would soon come for the remaining Shovlins. On April 10, 1929, Edgar had just finished eating dinner with his mother. As he got up to go upstairs to his bedroom, he turned to his mother and said, "Good night." After a brief pause, he turned back to his mom and strangely said, "Goodbye." Just a few minutes later, the deafening echo of a gunshot rang through the house. Several of the boarders ran to Edgar's room as Lucy frantically ran up the stairs.

They found Edgar lying in a pool of blood, the revolver still in his hand, his skull fractured from the bullet that had pierced through it. He lay unconscious in that dying condition until he could finally be moved to the hospital, where he was later pronounced dead. No one ever discovered why he had carried out this suicide. He left no note.

Now, the lovely home had two deaths on its floorboards.

The 1930 census shows Lucy lived alone at 404 East Commercial Avenue, and the home was valued at $40,000. She died on October 20, 1938, at the age of eighty-one. It is unclear if Lucy also died in the home.

Do the spirits of Dennis and Edgar still walk the halls and roam the rooms of their old family home? Does Edgar's grief and sorrow still linger in the room where he pointed a gun at his head and pulled the trigger?

Charles Simmons and his wife are shown to have been living at 402 East Commercial Street in 1924, but since the home still retained the 404 address, they may have resided at a smaller home located on the parcel.

Thomas Emmett Lyons (1884–1950) purchased the home next. Lyons was born in Michigan and moved to Anaconda in 1890. Thomas and Margaret Patricia Mclaughlin (1897–1967) were married in 1925 in Anaconda and are listed on the property's title from 1939 to 1960. Thomas worked for many years as a visitors' guide for the copper smelter in town. Thomas died on

November 18 at St. Ann's Hospital. His bereaved widow soon left Anaconda and headed for Seattle, Washington, in 1968 but died soon after.

The home's address changed from 404 to 402 sometime after 1960.

The next family who lived in the home were the Clarks, who remained there until 1968. Descendants of the Clarks have nothing but positive and loving memories of the home. Even after the home was sold, the Clarks continued to visit the home often, just to relive their wonderful memories. This proves that not all negative situations or energies override people's emotions. When a home is filled with love and laughter, does it ward off negative vibes? The Clarks never experienced anything frightening or disturbing in the home during their ownership.

Dan and Eleanor Ivankovitch purchased the home in 1993 and owned it until 1995.

The six-bedroom, two bathroom, almost four-thousand-square-foot home now sits vacant, deteriorating and desperately needing love and attention. The home has been listed for sale off and on over the years, but the amount of money and remodeling it would require are extensive. A local curiosity, the historic home has been the residence of many families.

Does Karen have a spiritual connection with the house on Commercial Avenue? Some people believe that when a person feels drawn to a particular building, area or object it is because they have lived there or owned it in a previous life. It is unknown without further investigation whether Karen Broussard, who moved to Anaconda, Montana, from Seattle, Washington, has a deeper connection to the house on Commercial Avenue. One thing is certain, however, Karen feels a deep and powerful draw to the home and absolutely loves it.

Is the home really haunted? Some undoubtedly say yes. Other say absolutely not.

Many who have lived in the home, the Clark family for instance, have nothing but loving and fond memories when they remember living in the beautiful home.

Do some think the home is haunted simply because it is a vacant, historic home that can be conceived as "creepy," since it is in disrepair and deploys a mystery? So many people have lived in the home over its one-hundred-plus years, it is hard to say, especially when you factor in all of the lodgers who rented rooms there all those years ago.

Not all spirits have to be dark; many are helpful, considerate and kind energies.

*Note: You can watch the YouTube video for* Ghost Town Terror *at: https://www. youtube.com/watch?v=cV9nQg2ZuKc.*

# 5
# GHOST TOWNS NEARBY

*I think that's probably the real reason I go to the graveyard. I'm not afraid*
*of seeing ghosts. I think I'm really looking for ghosts. I want to see them. I'm*
*looking for anything to prove that when I drop dead, there's a chance I'll be doing*
*something a little more exciting than decaying.*
—The Pigman; *John Conlan, character; Paul Zindel, author*

## BANNACK, MONTANA

Another one of the most haunted ghost towns nearby is Bannack, Montana.
Now owned by Montana State Parks and the Bannack Association, it is a
paranormal investigator's paradise. Ghost tours are available to anyone
brave enough to enter the century-old buildings that line the vacant main
street and walk past the cemetery and wooden gallows that were once used
for hangings.

Four ghosts are said to haunt the town, and all of them haunt the old
Hotel Meade. The spirit of Doctor John Singleton Meade, who purchased
the building and renovated it to be a hotel, still roams the halls and staircase,
refusing to leave his beloved venture. Two other ghosts, a mother and daughter
team, can also be seen moving through the roams. Ruthless murderer and
notorious outlaw Henry Plummer (once the sheriff of Bannack who was
later hanged there along with a few of his deputies) is said to still walk the

The first jail in Montana was built in 1862 and was located in Bannack. Old mine workings are pictured in background. *Library of Congress.*

streets, making sure everyone is minding their ways. Sounds of disembodied voices and crying can be heard throughout the buildings, along with eerie footsteps from the unknown.

Bannack, located near Grasshopper Creek, was once a going concern, with almost three thousand citizens prospering there. The town was founded in 1862, after one lucky gold miner named John White struck it rich on July 28 of that year. His pals Chas Revel and William Still also made a small fortune in Grasshopper Creek. Mrs. R.W. Ball was the first woman to record a gold mining claim (No. 6) in Montana on November 10, 1862. That same year, over $700,000 ($5 million today) worth of gold was pulled from the town. The gold found in Bannack was supposedly 99 percent pure. Soon, over four hundred eager miners (known as Pikes Peakers) swarmed to dig through the famous Grasshopper Diggins in search of their fortunes.

Soon, the sleepy little town was being overrun by hopeful prospectors, sex workers and merchants. John Manheim opened the town's first brewery in 1862. Cyrus Skinner opened his saloon in 1863 (where they would later hold criminal trials).

Hotel Meade was erected in 1876 and is now haunted by Dorothy Dunn and her mother, Sarah. *Library of Congress, item no. 2017815179; John Vachon, photographer.*

Bannack became official in 1863, when it was granted an official post office, and Dr. John Singleton Meade became its postmaster. It continued to attract its fair share of outlaws, bar owners and horse thieves, who brought much excitement to the once-quiet town. The first man to be hanged at Hangman's Gulch in Bannack was Pete Horoan. The second was R.C. Rowley in 1864.

In 1864, Bannack became the first territorial capital of Montana, but that was a short-lived title, as the county seat was moved to nearby Dillon in 1881.

The Hotel Meade has a long and fascinating history.

The two-story brick building was originally constructed in 1875 for $14,000 and became the first Beaverhead County Courthouse. In 1877, the hotel was barricaded by citizens who were hiding behind the safety of the brick walls, as they were terrified of an attack from the angry Nez Perce Natives.

The building sat vacant for several years until late 1890.

In 1891, Dr. John Singleton Meade decided to purchase the building and have it remodeled into an upper-class hotel with thirty comfortable and

The staircase in the Hotel Meade, where many have sighted the ghosts of Dorothy Dunn and her mother, Sarah, where they once lived and worked. *Library of Congress, item no. mt0001, Historic American Buildings Survey, Creator and Steele and Tasker.*

fashionable rooms. He demanded the staff serve food on only fine china and accompanied by crisp white linens. At the Hotel Meade, Singleton hosted major social events and parties.

But later, the hotel's delicate, patterned china and fancy white linens were replaced by bloody cots and stores of medical equipment, as it was used as a makeshift hospital for victims of the smallpox and typhoid epidemics.

In 1895, Percy Meade (whose parents were running the Meade Hotel at the time) went to work as usual at the Eugenia Mine in town. That fateful August night, he told his wife as he kissed her goodbye, "This is going to be my last shift underground." He was sure he was going to find better work soon and hoped for a nicer life for his family. Unfortunately, mud let loose down in the mine that night and quickly filled the south drift, suffocating Meade almost instantly. Could his also be one of the ghosts haunting the Meade Hotel?

In 1897, Meade had enough of the hotel business and offered it up for sale.

In 1940, the doors of the Meade Hotel were closed for good. The rest of the townsfolk left Bannack and its buildings in their rearview mirrors in the 1970s. Today, it is a ghost town and state park that attracts tons of visitors each year.

Does the ghost of Singleton still roam the halls and stairs of the Meade Hotel, never wanting to miss the next party at his fabulous hotel? Many think so. Perhaps Percy also hangs out with his father at the hotel.

## Drowned Girl Haunts the Hotel Meade

Another pair of ghosts suffer a tragic past. An extremely beautiful young girl, only sixteen years old, named Dorothy Dunn (1900–1916) died on August 4. Dorothy went to Grasshopper Creek to play in the water with her cousin Fern and her best friend Bertie Matthews (1897–1988). The three were playing and enjoying the sun when, suddenly, they stepped off a ledge hidden below the water of the pond.

Dorothy had no idea how to swim.

A young twelve-year-old boy named Smith Paddock and his friend Ruth Wornick were nearby and saw that the trio was in trouble. They quickly jumped in to try to help them to safety. Bertie and the cousin were pulled to shore and survived. Dorothy was not so lucky. When she was pulled to the

*Left*: A possible image of the beautiful Dorothy Dunn, who accidentally drowned at Grasshopper Creek and now haunts Hotel Meade. *Library of Congress, item no. 2018708044; Arnold Genthe, photographer.*

*Below*: Grasshopper Creek, where Dorothy Dunn drowned. *Library of Congress.*

shore, she was not breathing, and they were unable to resuscitate her. She was buried at Bannack Cemetery.

Dorothy's mother, Sarah, and her father, Ed Dunn, were completely devastated.

Dorothy spent most of her short life at the Hotel Meade, as her mother worked there. As their years at the hotel were some of their happiest, it is no wonder they never want to leave it. Their ghostly figures have been spotted in most of the rooms in the Hotel Meade.

Bertie took Dorothy's death very hard and never seemed to recover from it. Bertie's parents, Rufe and Montana Mathews, operated the hotel during the period that Dorothy and Sarah were working there. Bertie saw Dorothy's ghost many times lingering in the upstairs of the hotel. She is always seen wearing her favorite long, blue dress.

Bertie, who was born in Bannack, lived to be ninety-one years old. After Dorothy's death, she suffered the loss of both her brother Roy and her sister Hazel, who both tragically died from influenza. Her godson, Lee Graves, testified that Bertie told him she saw Dorothy's ghost in the upstairs rooms of the Meade on many occasions.

Dorothy and her mother continue to take care of and maintain the hotel, even in the afterlife.

*Note: Today, the townspeople of Bannack and Bannack State Park offer ghost walks and yearly fun events. It is considered the best-preserved ghost town in the state of Montana. Tours are conducted from the visitor center, which is open from Memorial Day through Labor Day. Bannack Days, with historic displays, reenactors and activities, are held annually during the third weekend in July. The park is located at 721 Bannack Road, Dillon, Montana, 59725, 406-834-3413. If you cannot travel to Bannack, you can enjoy a sneak peek video on their website at: https://fwp.mt.gov/stateparks/bannack/.*

## LEGENDARY BANDIT HENRY PLUMMER IS HANGED IN BANNACK

Another feisty spirit that haunts the ghost town of Bannack is that of the legendary outlaw Henry Plummer (1832–1864). He has his final resting place in Bannack.

Plummer sailed from New York to California alone when he was just a young lad. He landed in San Francisco, where he secured a job in a bakery.

He saved enough of his wages to move to Nevada City, California, where he bought a ranch and part of a mine. He then bought the Empire Bakery. By 1856, at the age of twenty-four, he had become the marshal of the third-largest settlement in the state of California.

In 1857, Plummer killed his first man. Henry was having an affair with the wife of a local miner named John Vedder, who did not take kindly to Plummer sleeping with his wife. Plummer shot him. He was convicted of second-degree murder and sentenced to ten years at the famous San Quentin Prison in 1859. He was quickly pardoned and was soon on his way.

In 1862, Plummer checked into the well-known Luna House in Lewiston, Idaho. That same year, he made his way to Bannack, Montana, and was peacefully drinking whiskey in the Goodrich Saloon. But the peace was short-lived, and Plummer found himself in a tangle with a man named Jack Cleveland. The two started arguing, and Plummer pulled out his gun and shot Cleveland, who died three hours later. Although Plummer was arrested, he was tried and acquitted by the jury; they considered the shooting one done in self-defense.

The townsfolk must have had some trust in Plummer, as in 1863, they elected him Bannack's sheriff. He quickly built the first jail, a hardy wooden building that had iron rings imbedded into the floor, a convenient way to chain an outlaw down so they couldn't break out.

Some records indicate Plummer was an all-around great guy; others suggest he was one of the most vile, temperamental and mean men they had met. It is recorded that women found Plummer irresistible. Local miners claimed he terrorized their community and was a vicious murderer.

Bannack had a population of seven hundred in 1879. Locals frequented such places as the Skinner Saloon, the Masonic temple and, of course, the Hotel Meade.

Plummer was said to have run a gang of over one hundred ruthless men in a band called the Innocents. There was a dusty wagon trail that led from Virginia City to Bannack, and road agents and miners used it to haul copper, ore with gold shipments and other valuables. This road was one of the most dangerous around, and over one hundred men were murdered en route.

Although Plummer was elected sheriff of Bannack in 1863 at the age of twenty-seven, many believed he was really an outlaw—and the one responsible for many of the robberies committed on the famous road in the 1860s.

A group of men formed their own band of protection in Virginia City and called themselves the Vigilante Committee. They were determined to catch and hang the robbers. Between 1863 and 1864, they were responsible for hanging between twenty-three and twenty-five men!

Rumors began to circulate again that Plummer himself was responsible for the thefts. A group of men rounded up Plummer and his two deputies, Buck Stinson and Ned Ray. They were determined to hang all three men. On January 10, 1864, they all hanged from the very gallows Plummer had built for another criminal. Supposedly, he yelled out, "I will tell you where $100,000 in gold is buried if you let me live!" Right before the floor dropped and he was left to swing from the noose, he begged, "Please give me a good drop."

All three men were buried in shallow graves at Hangman's Gulch, just one hundred yards from the gallows. A local cabinet maker named George French was hired to construct Plummer's casket. He was paid $42.50 for the coffin and his burial.

Grave robbers soon ravaged the area in search of collectibles. One was a doctor who was obsessed with having the arm off Plummer in order to get the bullet that was lodged in it from a prior injury. So, he took his arm.

Two drunk men, on a dare, dug up Plummer's body and took his skull. They carried it back to the Bank Exchange Saloon, where it sat on the back bar for years until the place burned down. Another unlikely rumor is that Plummer's skull was sent off to a university so students could discover what made Plummer so evil.

To this day, some historians feel they can prove that Henry Plummer was no outlaw and that his hanging was wrong. They have been able to find no concrete evidence that Plummer committed any crimes in relation to the robberies.

Directions: Bannack State Park is located in the southwestern area of Montana. Take I-15 south of Dillon to exit 59 (Highway 278 exit). Drive west on Highway 278 for eighteen miles. Turn south onto the Bannack Bench Road and travel for four miles. The park entrance road will be on the left-hand side.

*Note: Bannack hosts a ghost walk in late October. Call 406-834-3413 for more information.*

# A GHOST TOWN CALLED GARNET

Another nearby ghost town is Garnet, and it rests near the First Chance Gulch at the base of Anaconda Hill. The town has thirty buildings and has been left mostly untouched over the years. The old buildings still stand as a testament to the once-thriving city. Since its takeover in 1970, the Bureau of Land management has maintained the property.

Some people say they have seen the apparition of a man in cowboy gear roaming the town's streets late at night. The eerie sounds of piano music from Kelly's Saloon can often be heard around midnight, but no pianos remain intact there. The sounds of disembodied male voices can be heard from many of the buildings, but as soon as someone approaches the structures, the voices stop. Others have seen ghostly footprints in fresh snow when no one else is around. The apparition of a female ghost is often seen as she peers out the upstairs window of the Wells Hotel. The legend of the female apparition is that she was a local pioneer whom some believed was a witch. When she became accused of murder, she was executed.

The town of Garnet (formerly Mitchell) was founded in 1895, when Samuel Ritchie, considered the founder of Garnet, discovered the "Nancy Hank" (Abraham Lincoln's mother's name) Lode just west of Garnet. Soon, Dr. Armistead Mitchell constructed a stamp mill to crush the ore found near First Chance Gulch. Many of the miners began moving their picks and packs from Granite County to Garnet in search of their fortunes. Garnet was officially established in 1895 and opened its post office in 1896. In 1897, the town was officially called Garnet. By 1898, the town's population was around one thousand.

The town was devastated when a fire broke out on October 4, 1912, and burned down almost all its structures. It broke out in one of the many saloons, its initial flame left undiscovered. The only buildings that remained after the fire were one store, a saloon and a small hotel.

The town continued to rebuild and prosper until World War I, when many men had to go off for the war. Davey's General Store and the Wells Hotel remained open and continued to operate.

When gold prices rose around 1934, many miners returned to Garnet, and the population went up to 250.

One of the most prominent citizens of Garnet was Frank Davey. He opened his general store in 1898, and it continued to operate until his death in 1947. He also owned the blacksmith shop, a stagecoach line (that offered the luxury of buffalo robes for warmth when traveling) and a hotel.

Adjoining his store was a place where one could weigh gold, butcher meat and buy hardware. At the time of his death, Davey owned the entire town and most of the land. His heirs donated everything they could to the United States government.

During its heyday, Kelly's Saloon was the place to go for a cold beverage or shot of whiskey. The one-and-a-half-story building was thirty by twenty feet and boasted three rooms on the second floor, possibly for sex workers to board in. It was formerly the Bob Moore Saloon, until L.P. Kelly bought it in 1898 for $1,500. It is said piano music was always playing at the saloon to entertain its patrons, and the music can still be heard (even though no one is at its keys) every night at midnight.

Wells Hotel was also a favorite spot in town. The two-and-a-half-story hotel was built in 1897 by John Wells and was one of the largest in town, fifty by thirty feet. The glamorous Mrs. Winifred Wells lovingly designed the hotel, and it featured elaborately carved doors, an elegant oak staircase, beautiful stained-glass windows, a ladies' parlor and a grand dining room. One would think that the ghostly apparition of a woman peering out the windows of the Wells Hotel could be none other than Winifred herself, still carefully tending to her guests and her grand hotel. When the Wells Hotel closed its doors in the 1930s, Davey took over its kitchen.

The last resident to leave Garnet was a woman named Marion Dahl. Her old home still stands on Main Street in town. Ollie and Marion Dahl ran a speakeasy during Prohibition until 1933. Ollie was an architect and builder during his prosperous days in Granite. He promptly built the Dahl house and the Dahl Saloon. The saloon was a one-and-a-half story, twenty-four-by-twelve-foot building with a false front. The original part of the saloon was run by Mel Stairs before Dahl purchased it. It operated until the mid-1960s.

The fabulous ghost town now attracts many visitors each year, most hoping to get a glimpse of Winifred Wells herself, Mr. Frank Davey or even one of the old miners' ghostly apparitions.

# GARNET'S GHOSTLY SAND PARK CEMETERY

The tiny cemetery known as Sand Park served both Granite and nearby Coloma for a brief period. Granite is four miles to the east and Coloma is half-mile north of the gravesite. The cemetery's location is due to the ground conditions. Most of the land is very rocky and hard, whereas the small section selected for the graveyard is soft, sandy loam. Some claim it is haunted by the spirits from the unmarked graves.

No one knows for certain how many bodies are buried at Sand Park. The reason? Before World War II, the Works Projects Administration decided to create a road and plowed their bulldozers right through the middle of the graves. Soon, the workers realized that they were disturbing skeletal remains and found pieces of coffins.

A large hole was dug, and all of the dead bodies and coffins were placed inside of it, together making one mass grave. The disturbance of a grave can sometimes create negative energy, and the unsettled dead are now interrupted. Some say the sprits who were once lying peacefully in their graves are now roaming the area, awakened after being moved.

There are only six remaining undisturbed graves in the cemetery. The period in which the cemetery was actively used was from 1896 to 1914. The graves remaining belong to Tom Williams, William Ross, William Hamilton, William Scheehan, Frank Holmes and Mrs. Pete Shipler. Who were these early pioneers? Attempts to further identify them have been made through research, but whether the facts are completely accurate is undecided. The following is what we might know about the dead who are lying in the *undisturbed* graves:

No information has been found about Tom Williams.

William Ross died in late 1898, but prior to that, he was a very busy man. He filed a mineral claim near Coloma called the Buena Vista on September 27, 1898. He opened a saloon called the Halfway House on Granite Road in town. In March 1898, he bought a one-year lease for the Dunwoody Quartz Lode from R.A. Estey for $2,000. In May that same year, he worked under a lease for the Mollic Gibson claim, near Coloma.

William Hamilton lived from 1868 to 1905 and originally emigrated from Canada in 1887. The federal census from 1900 for Granite disclosed he was a quartz miner.

Although Frank Hamilton has no headstone, records indicate he was buried in the cemetery. He was approximately thirty-five years old and came from Colorado.

No information has been found about William Scheehan.

Frank Holmes died in 1914. He was originally from Sweden and was a quartz miner and saloonkeeper in town. He died of heart failure due to his alcoholism.

Mrs. Pete Shipler has what is perhaps one of the more fascinating graves. The marker states only "Mrs. Pete Shipler." Her maiden name was Katie

Blodgett (1875–1909, age thirty-four years) and she was born in Ravalli, Montana. When she was twenty years old, she married thirty-year-old Mr. William Peter Shipler (1865–1944, age seventy-nine) in Missoula, Montana, on July 16, 1895. Pete Shipler was originally from Pennsylvania. He actively worked the Copper Cliff Mine with Sam Adams, both men well known in Anaconda. The marriage was tested in 1903, when their young daughter, Maude (1896–1903), died. It was tested again in 1907, when Katie filed for divorce on the grounds of "desertion, neglect and failure to provide." Mr. Shipler, at the time, was supposedly worth $10,000, and she was asking for only $50 per month in alimony. He contested the divorce, but eventually, the divorce was granted.

Pete was remarried in 1940 to Pearl Moog. He continued to work in Granite on a part-time weekend basis. Some records indicate that Katie was remarried in 1908, one year before she died, but the facts on several accounts are conflicting. It is sad to note that her lonely grave marker reads only "Mrs. Pete Shipler." It does not state her date of birth or death, nor even her own name, only the name of a man who deserted her and left her lonely. Perhaps if there is a female ghost roaming the Sand Park Cemetery, it is that of Katie searching for her husband.

Directions: Turn right off Highway 200 at milepost marker 22 onto Garnet Range Road. Continue for seven miles, going past the turn-off to Coloma. There is a sign for the cemetery.

# THE HAUNTED OPERA HOUSE THEATER

Established in 1891, the theater in Philipsburg, Montana, was originally called the McDonald Opera House and is located at 140 South Sansome Street. The theater has been operating since its opening night, making it Montana's oldest continuously running theater.

Parts of the building have offered other services to locals over the years: a livery stable, a bank and even a soda pop bottling company. The interior of the building is grand, and its elaborate nature seems out of place in a little town of fewer than one thousand residents. The theater is considered one of the top ten most haunted theaters in the world. People who have visited the theater, as well as staff members, have reported their hair being pulled, feeling creepy cold spots, hearing phantom footsteps and smelling cigars. Images of ghostly faces and apparitions have also been seen throughout the building.

Who (or what) is haunting the theater?

Perhaps it is the town's founder, Philip Deidesheimer (1832–1916), who platted the parcel in 1867, a year after arriving in Philipsburg. Deidesheimer was a humble but brilliant mining engineer.

The parcel of land the theater now stands on was originally purchased for the Northern Pacific Railroad in 1876. Later, in 1896, Angus McDonald and his wife, JoAnna, bought the land and began their dream of building an opera house on it. They even splurged for a granite foundation and plumbing.

In 1919, the building would change hands once again when Frank Horrigan purchased the opera house and renamed it the Granada.

The theater's current owners, Tim and Claudette Dringle, are lovingly renovating the building and are offering live professional performances for everyone to enjoy.

With so many former owners who poured their hearts and souls into the theater, it is hard to say who exactly is haunting the building. Perhaps when one catches a hint of cigar smoke while sitting in the audience, the ghostly face of the guilty party will be captured on film.

# A Murder Over Cards

Perhaps it is the ghost of Joseph Gird, who was killed in the street of Philipsburg in 1893, that continues to roam through the small town.

Although Philipsburg is not a ghost town, it is a quaint little spot where one can grab a coffee or eat a sandwich on their way through.

The sad story begins in the late 1890s.

J.W. Brown and Joe Gird rode into Phillipsburg on horseback, their throats dry and muscles tired. They tied their horses up near the Flint Station and then walked over to Brown's Saloon for a cold one. The men were so thirsty that it took three rounds to finally quench their thirst. As Gird felt around in his pockets, he discovered only $1.25 in them.

"I have $1.25 left," he told the men, "I wanna play poker for it!"

That sounded like a swell idea, so the men sat down to play cards. Another man, James Campbell, also sat down to play. After a few hands, Campbell and Gird decided it was time to move on. As Gird left the saloon, he yelled back to Brown, "You had the best of me once with the Henry rifle, didn't you, Brown?"

Whatever prior disagreement the men had was a mystery to Campbell and anyone else in the saloon.

Soon, Brown pulled out his gun and began shooting at Gird. The first bullet hit him in his left breast. The second bullet entered through Gird's back. Gird tried to get on his horse and ride off into the sunset, but soon, he fell out of his saddle and hit the dusty road.

The coroner T.G. Heme was called, and he told the crowd that Gird had suffered from a hemorrhage caused by the bullet in his back that had cut through his pulmonary artery.

Brown was sentenced to ten years in Montana State Prison for second-degree murder. It could be the ghost of either Gird or Brown that haunts the streets of Philipsburg.

## Virginia City: The Most Haunted Town in Montana

One of Montana's most haunted (and most famous) ghost towns is Virginia City. Although it is a day's drive from Anaconda (ninety-seven miles), it is well worth the trip. Nearly every building in the town has a story to tell and a ghost lurking in its shadows. Some claim they refuse to walk the street at night because they are so likely to encounter a ghost.

The town dates to 1863, when Bill Fairweather and Henry Edgar discovered gold near Alder Creek. The town was essentially lawless, and robbers soon realized they could get away with murder—literally. In 1864, the town was full of five thousand hungry and thirsty people.

The Fairweather Inn, at 307 West Wallace Street, is haunted by a slew of ghostly children who love to play games, pull hair and basically cause chaos. Room no. 10 is reportedly the most haunted of all. Established in 1863, the building has been used a butcher shop and was previously called the Anaconda Hotel and Saloon.

The town's bizarre past is rich in history, legends and lore, all of which make it one of the most fascinating destinations to explore. It is said the ghostly apparition of a soldier dressed in a Civil War uniform can be seen smoking a cigar late at night.

The Bonanza Inn is located one block off Main Street and was built in 1866; it also served as the county courthouse. Later, three nuns turned it into a St. Marys' Hospital for miners. Sister Irene's spirit is reported to be the ghost that still lingers in the building, unable to let go of her past. Strange odors and noises can often be heard in the building. Irene loved her patients and the hospital so much, she now refuses to leave. Room no. 1 is supposed to be the most haunted.

Around 1940, the town fell into disrepair, and two highly motivated people, Charles and Sue Bovey, bought much of the town and began the lengthy process of restoration and preservation. They purchased both the Fairweather Inn and the Bonanza. Later, the state purchased most of Boveys' properties and has maintained the town ever since.

One of the most horrific events that occurred in Virginia City took place on January 14, 1864. A team of vigilantes were sick and tired of the rampant crime and created a long list of twenty-four men who needed to be hanged. They called their list the "Yeager's list." They quickly rounded up a group of criminals, eager to hang them. Five of the men who were captured and hanged that day in 1864 were:

1. Jack Gallagher, a known robber and murderer.
2. Club-foot George Lane, a dirty telegraph agent for Henry Plummer.
3. Hayes Lyons, a known robber and murderer.
4. Frank Parish, a stage coach robber and murderer who also worked for Henry Plummer.
5. Boon Helm, the worst of the group, who was a known murderer and cannibal.

All five men were marched down Wallace Street, right up to the beam that had been erected specifically for this purpose. Many claim the spirits of these five men (and many others) are the ghosts that still roam the streets of Virginia City, Montana, smoking, pinching girls' bottoms and drinking phantom whiskey.

# 6

# PIONEERS WHO REFUSE TO LEAVE

*I know a few things about ghosts. The only way to stop them getting inside you is*
*to spend every second of the day thinking about something else.*
*Fighting like that makes you tired, and it doesn't matter how hard you fight*
*anyway. They chip till they make a crack, and before you know it,*
*there's a ghost squatter in your living room. It's hard to get them out. Hard*
*because they settle in. Hard because you like the company.*
*—Cath Crowley*

The history of old towns is fascinating, and it is important to remember those who strove to build up the city, establish their homes and businesses and even rebuild if needed after a fire. So many early pioneers are forgotten, their lives nothing more than an old advertisement placed in the *Anaconda Standard* or a message scratched on a crumbling tombstone.

Some of the earliest pioneers and businessmen of Anaconda from 1896 are Dr. Chrisman (the local dentist), Charles Lane (architect) and Reverend Hawkins.

Would anybody remember D.G. Brownell from 1899, the proprietor of the Anaconda Livery Stable located on the corner of Stable and Office Streets (who also ran the Passenger, Baggage and Express line for the trains)? How about MacCallum and Clouter, the local grocers who sold shoe polish, fresh vegetables and pure malt extract? If a citizen of Anaconda was looking for a home to purchase, they would visit realtors Smith and Mahoney. They offered a five-room modern house with a bathroom on a good-sized lot on

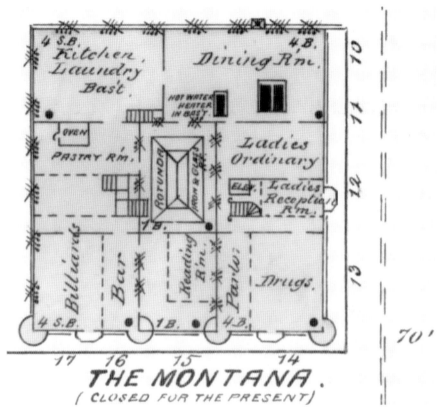

A Sanborn map drawing of the layout of the ground floor of the Montana Hotel in 1890. The image shows a pastry room, a drugstore, a bar and a billiards room, among other facilities that were available. *Library of Congress.*

Locust Avenue for $1,700. Their office was located inside the Montana Hotel. W. Thornton sold fire insurance. Madame Young would cut and style your hair in her beauty parlor in room no. 5 in the Commercial Hotel.

All of these old pioneers helped build Anaconda. They worked hard, and most led simple lives. Others created tragedy and violence within the town's limits.

Why some spirits refuse to leave a location will always be an unsolved mystery. Do they have unfinished business they need to tend to? Are they seeking revenge for their murder? Or perhaps these restless spirits just hang around because they love Anaconda so much.

## MARCUS DALY: ANACONDA'S COPPER KING

One of the most prominent Anaconda citizens and early pioneers was Marcus Daly. Not only did he do everything he could to make the town what it is today, but he also went the extra mile. Daly was one of the legendary Copper Kings. It is no wonder that many people feel they have seen his ghostly images in various places around Anaconda and Butte. Why would someone who did so much for his city, county and state ever want to leave? He was loved by everyone who met him, made certain those he cared about were well taken care of and even provided for those he knew little of.

A photograph of Marcus Daly. *From the* Wolf Point Daily, *August 19, 1920.*

His legendary business sense started at a young age, when he began working at a store in New York City making fifty cents per week. He saved his wages until he had enough to gain passage to San Francisco, California. Then he was employed at Walker Brothers in Salt Lake City but quit in 1880.

His mentor was another historical legend, the famous George Hearst (1820–1891), an extremely wealthy American businessman, miner and politician. They met in Nevada, where Daly learned the mining business from him—and the men became friends. Daly and Hearst became partners and developed the Anaconda Mine.

In 1881, Daly purchased the Anaconda Copper Mine in Butte from Michael Hickey for $30,000 (with funding from his two pals, James B. Haggin and newspaper millionaire William Randolph Hearst [1863–1951], the son of George Hearst). Daly and his crew began the daunting task of digging a deep shaft. Although the mine produced silver, Daly was hot after copper. He believed that copper veins ran below water level—and he was right.

In 1882, Daly purchased a large strip of land on which he desired to build a smelter. This land later became known as Anaconda.

After making a hefty profit, Daly purchased the St. Lawrence Mine in Anaconda Hill for $162,500 in 1883. The St. Lawrence was profitable but had its stumbling blocks. Multiple fires and accidents plagued the mine. In 1891, the mine caught fire, and nine men were killed. A cage accident soon killed another nine men.

Do the restless souls of these eighteen men still haunt Anaconda Hill?

Daly built the Anaconda Smelting plant for $10 million and then the new Washoe Plant for another $5 million, pumping a lot of money into the small town. His smelter was producing eleven million pounds of copper per month. That brought the value of Anaconda to $20 million!

Although Daly was one of the richest men around, he was considered one of the kindest and most considerate. If a miner of his own was killed, Daly promptly met with his widow and family, and typically, he would give them some money and purchase a small home for their comfort.

In 1888, he began building his grand, European-style hotel on Main Street in Anaconda, simply called the Montana Hotel. Some believe Daly's spirit still roams his once-lavish hotel, now home to local businesses. Before the magnificent Montana Hotel was built, the best accommodations in town were at the Palace Hotel, a three-story, fifty-room brick building located on Front Street.

The hotel's bar was extensive and modeled after a bar in the old Hoffman House in New York. The hotel featured mahogany woodwork and details, and in the bar, the floor had a wooden inlay mosaic of Daly's favorite racehorse, Tammany. A hand-painted mural adorned the wall.

Hotel Montana was built by Marcus Daly in 1889 and was "thoroughly fire proof, has running water, baths, heat, elevators, fire alarms, fire places, and all modern conveniences." *Library of Congress, item no. 100239p.*

A beautiful interior photograph of the parlor room located at the east end of the Hotel Montana. *Library of Congress, item no. 100233p.*

It is said that Daly, when reaching the final stages of building the hotel, said to the contractor/architect D.F. McDevitt of Butte, "It doesn't look big enough. Put another story on it." And since money was not an issue for Daly, the contractors did as they were told and added an extra story, plus one more for the hell of it. It cost Daly $125,000 to build the hotel, and at the time, it was one of the most deluxe and comfortable hotels in Montana. It featured gas lighting and hot water in all the bathrooms. The fireplaces were carved from fine Italian marble. It even had steam heat.

Daly had a vision of Anaconda becoming the state's capital, but that venture never came to be.

When Montana became a state in 1889, Daly envisioned famous men, state and national politicians and other people of significance staying at his hotel.

The hotel opened with a bang and a lavish ball on July 4, 1889.

*Note: The hotel was renamed the Hotel Marcus Daly in 1962. It was closed in 1976, and two years later, in 1978, the top two stories were removed. Today, the once-glorious architectural feat still maintains its corner turrets, big arched windows and intricate brickwork, along with its name and details.*

Daly was also the owner and creator of the local newspaper, the *Anaconda Standard*, which he invested $30,000 in 1889 to establish. The first issue hit the streets on September 4, 1889.

Never tiring of a new adventure, Daly began raising racehorses, some of which were worth $50,000 each. He spent millions of dollars on his beloved horses, some of which he brought from as far away as Europe to compete in America. He was the owner of famous racehorses, such as Tammany, Hamburg, Ogden and other top stallions in the region. Daly was considered one of the finest all-around judges of horses in America.

The year 1892 kept Daly busy, as he soon ventured into building a new railroad. The Butte, Anaconda and Pacific Railroad cost him and his partners $4 million to construct.

When the news of Daly's death hit the papers, the entire state mourned. He was feeling ill while in Europe and was ordered to remain on bed rest. In the comforts provided by the staff at the Hotel Netherland on Fifth Avenue in New York City, Daly was surrounded by his family and closest friends. He was suffering from Bright's disease and a weak heart.

As Daly grew weaker, those he loved the most sat by his side: Mrs. Daly; Marcus Daly Jr. (and his brother Patrick); his daughters, Mary, Margaret and Harriet; Reverend M.J. Lavelle; and his personal attorney William Scalon. At 7:00 a.m. on November 13, 1900, his last words were, "Only a little while more, just a little bit more."

At the time of his death in 1900, his stocks and assets were worth $75 million ($479,434,686.50 today), and his cash was worth an estimated $15

*Above*: Several of Marcus Daly's favorite racehorses, Tammany, Ogden and Hamburg, running at a track in Hamilton, Montana, in 1910. *From the Western News, May 1, 1910.*

*Left*: Hotel Netherlands in New York City, where Anaconda pioneer Marcus Daly died in 1900. *Library of Congress, item no. 89709820, Stereo-Travel Co., circa 1909.*

The statue of Marcus Daly, a pioneer miner, was erected in Butte in 1906 by his fellow citizens in remembrance of his good deeds. *Library of Congress, item no. 2017724994; Arthur Rothstein, photographer.*

million ($102,736,004.25 today). Marcus Daly went from being a penniless immigrant to a multimillionaire in his fifty-eight years.

His body was taken from the Hotel Netherlands to his residence at 725 Fifth Avenue, just south of Fifty-Seventh Street in New York City.

Thousands of individuals mourned his death. Comments were published in various newspapers by people who knew Marcus Daly. They say it all about this great man.

> *He was a man of large brain and great energy. Self-educated and without the advantage of early training in the schools, he equipped himself magnificently for the work which was required in his great enterprises....His own labors contributed very largely to the wonderful growth of Montana, and he was one of the most prominent in developing the great resources of this state.*
> *—H.L. Frank*

> *The loss to Montana will be incalculable, as he was one of the great factors in the upbuilding and development of the great resources of this state.*
> *—A.J. Davis*

> *Mr. Daly was a most wonderful man, and everybody in the state knows the quality of his heart and mind.*
> *—W.L. Moyer*

> *His domestic life was very beautiful and his devotion to his family most noteworthy. There will never be but one Marcus Daly.*
> *—John Noyes Sr.*

It is no surprise that Marcus Daly is an Anaconda pioneer who wishes to never leave.

## LIZZIE BORDEN'S MAID MOVES TO ANACONDA

> *Then I laid down in the bed. I heard the city hall bell ring,*
> *and I looked at my clock, and it was eleven o'clock. I wasn't drowsing*
> *or sleeping. In my judgment, I think I was there three or four minutes. I*
> *don't think I went to sleep at all. I heard no sound;*
> *I didn't hear the opening or closing of the screen door. I can hear that*
> *from my room if anyone is careless and slams the door. The next thing*

*was that Miss Lizzie hollered, "Maggie, come down!" I said,*
*"What is the matter?" She says, "Come down quick, Father's dead,*
*somebody came in and killed him."*
*—from the testimony of Bridget Sullivan, Andrew Borden's family maid*

Of all the historical gruesome murders that have continued to haunt people, some of the most notoriously prominent crimes are the axe murders of Andrew (1822–1892) and Abby Borden (1825–1892) at 93 Second Street in Fall River, Massachusetts, on August 4, 1892. Even today, law students try to solve the famous unsolved murders.

Yet after the sensational trial ended and thirty-two-year-old Lizzie was acquitted in 1894 of the horrendous crimes, Bridget Sullivan (1874–1948), the family maid, decided to move on with her life and move away from all the horror of the murders.

Bridget was born in Cork, Ireland, in 1874 and immigrated to the United States in 1889, when she was just fifteen years old. She then landed in Rhode Island, where she remained for one year. After a brief stint in Pennsylvania, Bridget gained employment with Mrs. Reed in Fall River, Massachusetts. The same year, she began working as a domestic worker for the Borden family. She had been working for the Bordens for two years and nine months at the time of their murders.

Bridget's testimony was favorable to Lizzie, who, to show her gratitude, had given her money to visit her parents in Ireland. With the money Lizzie gave her, Bridget bought a farm in Ireland for her parents. But later, Bridget obtained a new passport under a false name and returned to America.

But how did Bridget end up in Anaconda, Montana? Bridget had a close friend named Minnie Green. The two girls had traveled to the United States together. After the Fall River murders, Bridget joined her friend Minnie in Montana to start a new life.

Bridget gained employment as a domestic worker for the George and Alice Winston family, who lived at 510 Main Street in Anaconda. Perhaps she answered an advertisement that was printed in the *Anaconda Standard*.

Records indicate that Bridget married a fellow named John Sullivan (no relation) in 1905 in Anaconda. They never had children. They lived a quiet life, with John working at the smelter in town. Bridget inherited $1,000 from her grandfather in Ireland, which was about the only excitement for them.

John Sullivan died in 1939 at the age of seventy-one. Shortly after John's death, Bridget moved in with her niece Mary (Bantry Tim) Sullivan at 112 East Woolman Street in Butte.

The marriage certificate for Lizzie Borden's ex-maid Bridget Sullivan. She married John Sullivan (no relation) from Ireland on July 17, 1905, in Anaconda. *From Ancestry and Library of Congress.*

While in Anaconda, Bridget never spoke of the gruesome murders or her previous life with the Borden family. But in 1942, when Bridget was seventy-three years old, Mrs. Green received an urgent telephone call from her. She said she thought she was dying from pneumonia and had a secret she wanted to share with Minnie before she passed away. Minnie traveled to see Bridget, but by the time she got there, Bridget had already passed the crisis of her illness and decided *not* to reveal her deathbed secret after all.

But upon her deathbed, in 1948, Bridget *did* reveal one small clue to the ghastly Borden crime. She told her sister that she knew for a fact Lizzie had murdered her father and stepmother, due to several personal reasons. She also said that Lizzie paid her handsomely to be elusive during the trial.

A few more rumors were flying around that may or may not be true:

- Andrew was getting ready to sign his will, and the new change would have cost Lizzie a lot of money. Andrew had also been providing gifts of real estate to Lizzie's stepmother's family, which was causing a lot of anger and tension.

- Bridget had falsified her testimony at trial to protect Lizzie from prosecution.
- Andrew Borden made sexual advances toward Lizzie and her sister, Emma, and Abby knew about these but did nothing to stop it, thus the murders were brutal. Abby had been dead for an hour prior to the killing of Andrew. Abby had suffered eighteen whacks, and Andrew had been bludgeoned eleven times, making his face unrecognizable.
- Some suggest a lesbian relationship existed between Bridget and Lizzie. (It is documented that Lizzie was probably a lesbian, which had to be kept under wraps during that era and was shunned by society.)
- Bridget told Minnie she worked for the Bordens at the time of the murders and said she liked Lizzie and often took her side during tensions that occurred in the Borden household. She also confessed that she "helped Lizzie out at the trial."
- Lizzie's lawyer strongly encouraged Bridget to go back to Ireland and stay there, never to return to the United States.

The full truth may never be known about who murdered Andrew and Abby Borden. Lizzie's story about being in the barn on that sweltering hot day eating a pear makes no sense whatsoever (plus, there was no disturbance in the dust inside the barn). Bridget's story about washing windows during the heat of the day also makes no sense. And certainly, she would have seen someone enter or leave the Borden house if she was just outside the residence, especially a person who would have been covered in blood.

Bridget was buried at Mount Olivet Cemetery in Anaconda, forever next to her husband, John.

One could wonder if Bridget Sullivan's restless spirit still roams Anaconda or Mount Olivet Cemetery, where she lies in her final resting place, wishing she did not take the truth about the Borden murders and Lizzie to her grave.

The following are some strange and interesting facts about the Borden murders and Bridget Sullivan:

- Some sleuths suggest that Lizzie hid the famous axe head in a menstrual bucket with bloody rags in the basement, knowing no person would dig into that mess. Officers did find a pail of bloodied towels, and (as Lizzie figured) they did not investigate its contents. Lizzie told Officer William Medley that the bloody bucket had been sitting there for "three or four days"; however, Bridget told Officer Medley she had not seen the pail.

- There seems to be multiple death certificates issued for Bridget, and each has different information and dates. Yet some of the names and dates are the same. Why?
- Bridget lied about her age when she married John Sullivan so she would not be older than him. Bridget stretched the truth about a lot of things. The marriage certificate lists her age as thirty-five, when she was actually forty-five at the time.
- Andrew Borden was very shrewd and stingy with his money. It is rumored he would cut off a deceased person's feet to make a shorter coffin, which saved him money. He was not very well liked in Fall River, some report.
- Some guests think the spirits of the murdered couple still roam the halls and rooms of their residence in Fall River, which is now a bed-and-breakfast.
- There is a plaque at the former George and Alice Winston home in Anaconda located at 510 Main Street. It notes that Bridget Sullivan was a domestic servant for the prominent family

# NEARBY HAUNTS AND HORRORS

## *Old Montana State Prison*

The old Montana State Prison is considered one of the most haunted places in the entire state. Now, it is a museum, open to the public for tours, but the creepy ghosts of prisoners are still very active there. People can visit the old prison for fun events, day tours and even ghost hunts.

The complex even attracted the attention of the *Ghost Adventures* crew. Zak Bagen and his team conducted a lock-in there, and the episode appeared on the Discovery Channel on August 29, 2015. Next, the show *Ghost Lab* did an investigation called "No Escape" that was aired on December 25, 2010. A few years later, in 2020, the Travel Channel filmed an episode there for its *Destination Fear* series.

Disembodied voices, scratches, lingering foul odors, faint screams for help, angry growls and signs of vertigo are common experiences for both paranormal researchers and tourists.

Deer Lodge County Courthouse was built in 1898 for $100,000, and county officials moved to their new building the next spring. *Library of Congress.*

The prison, located at 1106 Main Street in Deer Lodge, was built in 1871 and was in service for 108 years until its doors were closed in 1979. It was originally built by the hard labor of the convicts and cost $40,000 to construct. It had twenty-four-foot-tall thick sandstone walls. Once prisoners entered the massive complex, they knew they would probably never leave.

Within its very first month of operations, the prison was already overcrowded. The cells were a cramped six by eight feet, with no plumbing, heating, electricity or ventilation, and each held two men. The conditions there were horrible, but even if the prisoners complained, no one cared. Although only three unlucky men were executed there—Duncan McKenzie (1995), Terry Langford (1998) and David Dawson (2006)—over two hundred convicts died within the walls of the prison.

In 1908, a small riot occurred in the old prison. Four prisoners rushed the guards and tried to overtake them. W.A. Hayes, Oram Stevens, C.B. Young and George Rock attacked Warden Frank Conley. It was obvious that Conley was not a man to contend with, weighing over three hundred

George Rock partook in the deadly riot at the Montana State Penitentiary in 1908, and he was also responsible for the murder of Warden John Robinson. *From the* Anaconda Standard, *June 16, 1908.*

pounds with a .41-caliber pistol always tucked neatly at his side. In self-defense Conley drew his gun and shot at three of the men. Although they were injured, none of the prisoners died. Unfortunately, Deputy John Robinson was killed during the attack, and Conley suffered an injury that required over one hundred stitches.

Rock and Hayes were given death sentences for their actions. Rock was scheduled to hang on June 16, 1908. Hayes was scheduled for the noose on April 2, 1909. Strangely, both hangings were botched, and both failed. Was the supernatural hand of some unseen person responsible for botching the hangings? Maybe this is another reason Montana State Prison is so haunted.

George Rock, who partook in the riot at the Montana State Penitentiary on March 8, 1908, was responsible for the murder of Deputy Warden John Robinson. Rock formerly lived in Jordan, Montana, and was already in trouble for killing a man named Ed Corl. Before his execution, Rock was provided comfort by Father Moran of Anaconda.

The scaffolding was erected in the northeast corner of the prison yard, and over two hundred spectators showed up, mostly friends of the deputy who wished to see Rock pay for his crime. The trapdoor was sprung, but the noose failed to tighten properly. For a long, gruesome eight minutes, horrified onlookers watched as Rock continued to twitch and struggle. Nervously, Dr. Girard kept checking the prisoner's pulse, praying for his death. Finally, after another few minutes and much throat clearing and glancing down at the floor, the botched process worked, and poor Rock was finally still.

William A. Hayes requested that his execution go smoothly, without any glitches. It was recorded in the *Butte Daily Post* on April 2, 1909, that Hayes said; "Try and make a good job of this if you can, sheriff, as I do not want to suffer any more than is necessary." Sheriff Joe Neville tried to assure the prisoner that he would do all in his power to have the execution move speedily and smoothly, and he said he hoped Hayes's neck would be broken when the weight fell.

Hayes was also involved in the riot at the Montana State Penitentiary on March 8, 1908. He was involved in the killing of Head Guard John Robinson and the serious wounding of Warden Frank Conley.

Rock, Hayes and another inmate named Stevens desperately wanted to escape the prison. During the scene, Hayes tried to place a wire loop around Conley's neck to strangle him. Conley quickly pulled his revolver and shot Hayes twice. Hayes drew a small knife and proceeded to stab at Conley. Rock continued to attack Deputy John Robinson. Robinson succumbed to his six deep wounds.

Robinson was born on August 1, 1853, and was considered one of the best men in the department. He had captured several murderers during his twelve years on the prison force.

Hayes's execution was also a failed attempt. Who or what was making this happen? It defied all logic, as the ropes, scaffolding and weights were all checked multiple times by various members of the team.

As the black cap was put over Hayes's head, the leather straps were tightened around the prisoners' arms and legs. Sheriff Neville tapped the canvas screen twice, signaling that all was a go. The calm executioner Beaton nodded politely and then quickly cut the rope that held the heavy weight. What should have been an instant death also resulted in the prisoner suffering while the others watched, unable to do anything to provide relief to Hayes.

Hayes's arms and legs twitched, and all the muscles in his body seemed to strain under the pressure. For a full five minutes, everyone stood by in complete shock. The doctor checked the man for a pulse and dropped his head. No words needed to be spoken, as they all silently knew this meant Hayes's neck had not been broken, and for another harrowing three minutes, Hayes was slowly strangled.

A few minutes later, four men in striped jail outfits moved toward the hanged man, carrying a black pine coffin. Beaton gently lowered the dead prisoner into the wooden box, and then the lid was screwed on tight. The makeshift pallbearers then slowly lifted the coffin and made their way over to the hearse that was waiting just outside the prison's gate.

## A Haunted Scaffold?

Many paranormal researchers feel that the scaffolding that remains at the old Montana State Prison is plagued by the residual energy of those who met their untimely death there.

Hayes was the tenth prisoner who met his fate on the "traveling" scaffold.

The first man was Frank Scott, who was executed in 1888.

The scaffold was dismantled and reassembled all over the state of Montana during its years of use. The condemned prisoners were not dropped, as was typical; instead, they were jerked into the air about three feet by a weight that weighed three hundred pounds.

## The Haunted Prison Theater

In 1920, local Copper King William Clark felt the prisoners needed some entertainment to lift their spirits. Clark was a good friend of Warden Conley's. He donated $10,000 toward the construction of a theater in the prison, which was completed in 1920. The grand establishment could comfortably seat one thousand people.

Today, the Montana State Prison Theater is haunted by the ghost of "Turkey Pete." His real name was Paul Eitner (1877–1967), and he was sentenced to life in the prison for shooting Joseph Nugent with his .38-caliber pistol on January 21, 1918, while living at a boardinghouse and working as a cook in Miles City, Montana.

Eitner was a German immigrant who eventually made his way to New Jersey. There, he was told by a doctor that he had tuberculosis and needed to move to a better climate or he would be dead in six months. That brought Eitner to Montana, where he worked at a military ranch. There, a cranky horse kicked him in the head and caused some brain damage.

After Eitner's short stint as a cowboy, he began working at a liquor store and acquired a drinking problem.

In 1918, Eitner began working as a cook in Miles City, Montana. He lived modestly in a boardinghouse with several other people, one being a cute woman named Miss Hope Mathena. Reportedly, another boarder named Joseph Nugent also had his eyes on Hope. Eitner's jealousy caused Nugent to get three bullets in his stomach and die three days later.

Turkey Pete was a short man, standing at just five feet tall, and he started his life behind bars when he was forty years old. Before he earned the nickname Turkey Pete, everyone called him "Shorty."

In 1992, Turkey Pete was granted the opportunity to work off-site and help feed, care for and raise the prison's turkeys. When a nearby farmer stopped by to admire the handsome turkeys, Paul offered to sell them to him for fifty cents each. Since they were not his turkeys to sell, this caused

Turkey Pete to lose his "job" caring for the turkeys—and earned him the new nickname "Turkey Pete."

Turkey Pete was harmless (well, except for that *one* man he murdered in cold blood), and everyone in prison liked him. He developed good friendship with other prisoners, as well as the staff. He would read the paper daily to others. His jail door was never locked, and he could come and go as he pleased, which was nice, since his cell (the same as everyone's) was only six by eight feet with a single light bulb.

But Turkey Pete's mental faculties were slowly deteriorating. The guards noticed he was confused often and lived in a fantasy world. Turkey Pete thought he had millions of dollars and owned thousands of acres of land. To entertain the fantasy, the prison print shop made false checkbooks for Pete. His new business name was Eitner Enterprises Inc. And since he had "billions" of dollars in his checking account, Pete would send money all over the world to help out those less fortunate. (Of course, these checks never left the prison walls.) He wrote a check and "bought" the Montana State Prison (and wrote the staff monthly checks for their salaries). He sent $125 million to President Kennedy to help out during the Cuban Missile Crisis. Another $10 million was sent to fight a raging fire in Brazil. For income, Turkey Pete

The William Clark Theater inside the Montana State Prison is haunted by Turkey Pete and several other ghosts. *Courtesy of Tananko, creative commons, Wikimedia.*

sold 10,000 of his pink alligators for $10 million so that he could purchase 1.5 million sheep for $2 zillion dollars.

Fellow inmates liked to play along and would write letters to Pete that supposedly came back from the people who received the funding, thanking him for his generosity. Even Fidel Castro received $9 billion for a large shipment of grasshopper legs.

Amid all this fun, Turkey Pete's health was deteriorating, along with his mind. After almost fifty years in jail, Turkey Pete finally died on April 4, 1967, at the age of eighty-nine. That's not too bad, considering they gave him only six months to live decades earlier.

His funeral was held inside the prison's theater and was the only funeral to ever be held there. Hundreds of mourners showed up to pay their respects to Turkey Pete. His cell, no. 1 in the 1912 cellhouse, was never used again and remained empty.

The famous Turkey Pete was buried at Hillcrest Cemetery on the prison grounds. He will also be loved and remembered as the man who generously donated zillions of dollars to those in need.

It is no wonder his restless spirit never wants to leave the old Montana State Prison.

When he was alive, any chances of parole were denied automatically, as it was obvious Pete could never function in the real world again. When asked what he would do if he ever got out of prison, he simply said, "Where would I go? This is my home."

It certainly is, Pete. And continues to be his ghost home to this day.

## *A Prison Riot Gone Wrong*

It is said the old Montana State Prison is also haunted by the spirits of several inmates who were killed during the 1959 riot. The tension started when prisoner Jerry Myles attacked Deputy Warden Ted Rothe. Prisoners Lee Smart and Donald Toms continued to attack the guard. Smart pulled out a rifle and shot Rothe in the chest, killing him instantly, and then he stabbed another guard. The prisoners soon gathered eighteen hostages, threatening to kill them all by lighting them on fire if their demands weren't met.

Myles, Smart and another prisoner named George Alton had control over the entire facility for thirty-six hours, beginning on April 16. They continued to throw gasoline on guards and threatened to burn them to death by lighting them on fire if they refused to cooperate in any way.

The three men were huddled together in cell block no. 1, planning their next move.

The entire riot soon got out of hand, and the national guard was brought in to get the prison back under control. Armored trucks began arriving on the grounds, with 150 heavily armed soldiers surrounding the perimeter. But Myles and Smart would not surrender.

*Boom!* The deafening sound of a bazooka being fired by National Guardsman Bill Rose filled the air. The target was the northwest corner of tower no. 1, where Myles and Smart were standing. The bazooka damaged the strong tower walls (the damage can still be seen today), and immediately, a second bazooka was aimed at the tower and fired. Then a blast came from a Thompson submarine gun that was fired by Patrolman Bob Zaharko through a window close to where the criminals were standing. Next, tear gas canisters were tossed at the men, followed by another blast from the bazooka.

Myles and Smart were lovers and made a pact to always be together, no matter what. They agreed to a murder/suicide pact if things came to that.

Inside, the panicked men felt they had no choice. Their fatal pact would have to be executed. Smart pointed the gun at his lover's head and fired. He then aimed the gun at his own head and pulled the trigger. Smart was just nineteen years old when he died. Myles was forty-four years old.

This gruesome scene took place at the top of the tower stairs, where ghostly apparitions still appear.

Part of Jerry Myles's jawbone was scattered during the murder/suicide, and someone picked it up and kept it as a souvenir for years. Some claim it is now at the museum as part of an exhibit. If his jawbone is there, it could hold residual energy from his death, which would cause him to haunt the place where he died so violently.

After the riot, the guards decided things had gotten a little loose around there and that they needed to tighten up the ship. They conducted constant searches of the prisoners. They even had the bodies of Myles and Smart wheeled around in front of the others so they could see the bloody corpses before they were sent to the coroner.

Lee Smart was born in Washington in 1940. He was convicted of the second-degree murder of a traveling salesman named Charles Ward in Montana on April 28, 1956. He robbed Ward of one hundred dollars and then beat him to death with a large pair if plyers. This murder got him thirty years at Montana State Prison.

Jerry Myles was born in Sioux City, Iowa, in 1915. His real name was Donald Groat. His life started out badly and just got worse. His mother was a homeless person who had no interest in raising a baby, so she gave him up for adoption. For his entire life, Myles was in and out of prison, a classic career criminal. He had a fairly high IQ, registering between 125 and 147. Yet he never put his intelligence to good use, and in 1945, he was sent to Alcatraz, where he would spend the years between 1945 and 1952 on the rock. He was then moved from Alcatraz to Leavenworth Prison in Kansas before he was then moved again to Georgia State Prison, where he was confined until 1958. He bragged about his bravado to other inmates, learning tips and tricks along the way about how to break out, how to manipulate guards and how to get his way.

When he was finally released from prison, he hopped a bus to Butte, Montana, where he immediately committed burglary and was again arrested. This was how he ended up at Montana State Prison.

Many paranormal investigators and visitors feel that the spirits of both Myles and Smart still haunt the tower where they died. Heavy footsteps and disembodied male voices are often heard. Visitors also report feeling despair, panic and anxiety when standing on the steps of the tower.

Over two hundred people died at the old Montana State Prison—it is no wonder it is one of the most haunted places in Montana.

*Note: The Discovery Channel's show* Ghost Lab *filmed a paranormal investigation at the location that aired on December 25, 2010. The Travel Channel's show* Ghost Adventures *filmed a paranormal investigation at the location that aired on August 25, 2015. The Travel Channel's show* Destination Fear *filmed a paranormal investigation at the location that aired on May 13, 2020.*

## A Prisoner Bakes to Death in the "Hole"

Montana State Prison got even more horrifying. In 1968, a twenty-six-year-old prisoner named Larry Cheadle would find his dreadful fate. Born in Wyoming in August 1940, Cheadle was caught and arrested for "using an automobile without the owner's consent." In 1961, Cheadle was sentenced to three years at Montana State Prison for his short-lived joy ride. He managed to escape his cell on August 30, and that earned him another year in jail.

The reason is unclear, but Cheadle was forced down into the hole as punishment by the guards. There were three solitary confinement cells in the complex. They each had a dirt floor, were unlighted, offered no ventilation and were located beneath the prison building. The steam pipes also ran through their walls, making the heat inside the holes unbearable. The prisoners were allowed the comfort of a dirty mattress, and a bucket was provided for them to use as a toilet. For nourishment, they were given one cup of water and one slice of stale bread three times per day.

At that point, the hole had not been used for some time. Records do not indicate why Cheadle was sentenced to the hole. The hole had sat closed and unused for several years before the Cheadle incident, so why was it reopened?

Unfortunately, Cheadle did not last even one day down there. After he was thrown in, he was found dead just six hours later. It was believed that he had actually died from burning up inside, as the heat was so extreme. On Halloween night, October 31, 1966, Larry Cheadle would take his final breath. His death was kept a secret by the prison until Cheadle's mother, Janet Sirrine, filed a wrongful death suit against the state and five prison officials in October 1967. She requested $250,000 for the death of her child, a small price to pay for his untimely murder.

Dr. John Newman performed an autopsy. His findings indicated that Cheadle had died from "acute pulmonary edema due to acute dilatation of the heart and possible epileptic seizure."

The Montana State Prison closed the holes for good after Cheadle's death. It was later exposed that Cheadle had a heart condition and should never have been placed in such a dangerous situation to begin with.

One of the most gruesome of prisoners was sent behind bars at Montana State Prison in 1970. Murderer, druggy and self-confessed cannibal Stanley Deanbaker was sentenced to life in prison for his horrific crimes. In 1970, he brutally killed two innocent men and was arrested on July 13. His first victim was forty-year-old Robert Salem. Salem was a lighting designer living in San Francisco, California. He had been repeatedly stabbed with a knife in April. Deanbaker's second victim was twenty-two-year-old James Schlosser. He was murdered in July by Deanbaker. His mutilated body was found when a fisherman snagged his line on a body in the Yellowstone River. Schlosser's heart had been crudely removed, and he was missing several fingers.

When Deanbaker was arrested, he admitted to eating Schlosser's heart. He also had Schlosser's finger bones tucked inside his shirt pocket. On his person, Deanbaker carried a recipe for LSD and had a copy of the Satanic Bible with him.

While serving his time behind bars, Deanbaker managed to make eleven crude weapons and continually threatened the lives of the guards. He was active in worshipping the devil and made no attempt to hide his actions. The worst part of the whole scenario is that in 1985, Deanbaker was released from prison. After his release back to Wyoming, he began living his life behind the scenes, his whereabouts hidden from the public for fear of *his* safety.

## Grant-Kohrs Ranch at Deer Lodge

Grant-Kohrs Ranch at Deer Lodge was purchased by the National Park Service in 1970. It is haunted by the ghosts of cowboys past and Augusta Kohrs.

The ranch was started by Richard Grant and his sons, John and James, and there, they ran cattle. In 1865, the local Natives burned down Grant's barn and stole all his cattle. This was enough for the Grant family, and they decided to leave Montana and the Natives behind. Richard sold the ranch to his friend Conrad Kohrs for $19,200 in 1866. He hoped it would make his new bride, Augusta, happy. And it did. The ranch was run by the Kohrs family until 1970.

Reports of phantom sounds of grain buckets rattling and cowboys talking and the sweet smell of lavender (Augusta's favorite perfume) are common. Strange handprints are often left on mirrors that have just been cleaned, doors have been seen opening and closing by themselves and the sounds of children's laughter have been heard by many people.

## Old Montana State Hospital

Many claim that the old Montana State Hospital near Deer Lodge is haunted. It is certainly old enough to house a few active ghosts. Founded by the territorial government in 1877 (twelve years before Montana became a state), it was also called the Warm Springs Hospital. It housed psychiatric patients, many of whom never left the grounds. After they died, they were simply buried in one of the hospital's two on-site cemeteries.

During the early 1920s, the staff at the hospital determined it would be good practice to sterilize some of the patients. They forcibly sterilized 11 patients against their will, and another 256 were made sterile between 1923 and 1954. In the 1950s, the facility housed around 2,000 patients.

## Butte–Silver Bow Courthouse

Just twenty miles from Anaconda sits a large brick building that housed many Montana criminals in its day and continues to be occupied by staff now. The original courthouse was built in 1884, and the new one was built in 1912 for the cost of $750,000!

The courthouse, located at 155 West Granite Street in Butte, is haunted by a murderer named Miles Fuller. Fuller was executed by hanging for his nasty deed of killing a fellow prospector named Henry Gallahan. Gallahan was born in 1850, served in the Civil War and was a member of the Lincoln post of the Grand Army of the Republic. He was only fifty-six years old when Fuller took his life. Gallahan lived peacefully in a small cabin by McKinley School. Fuller had tried to murder him before by putting shards of glass in his flour and strychnine in his sugar bowl. No one really knew why Fuller was out to get Gallahan, and his secret went to his grave with him.

Gallahan had been shot multiple times, and then his throat was slashed from ear to ear. Witnesses saw Fuller running from the site, and Sheriff Quinn quickly caught the killer.

On the morning of his execution, Fuller desired some hot coffee and some whiskey. At 4:15 a.m., Reverend Gwynne went to Fuller's cell, and they prayed together. Fuller would have to anxiously wait until 5:32 a.m. for his hanging. He maintained he was innocent until his neck snapped. His final words were, "Oh, my God!" His execution was one of the quickest recorded in Montana. After the masked man walked up to the scaffolding, Fuller told him, "Goodbye, I will meet you in Heaven." The masked man released the rope, and Fuller's body lurched upward. Dr. Tremblay checked Fuller for a pulse. There was none. They let his body hang from the rope for another eight minutes while the large crowd of morbid onlookers stared at it.

Fuller was not the only one executed by hanging on that scaffold. Dan Lucey, Dotson, McArthur, Potts, Metzger, James Martin and Tom Sing had all previously swung from the same rope.

Ghostly footsteps, cries for help and loud banging can be heard once in a while at the courthouse. Are these strange noises made by the spirits of the men who were hanged in the vicinity? Or is it something more sinister? Some claim it is the ghost of the masked man, the one who was in charge of releasing the rope, causing instant death for the men.

## *The Weeping Woman*

The apparition of a female spirit has been seen by numerous witnesses. Her presence always occurs in the same spot, a small cabin near Fish Creek, about half an hour outside of Anaconda.

Who is this woman, and why is she seen always weeping?

No one knows.

One man, Burt Duckworth, decided he would like to figure out the mystery once and for all. Duckworth and five of his buddies headed out to the cabin, determined to debunk the ghost story, as they were all firm nonbelievers. The men took a camera and other objects, like flashlights, to hopefully gain either evidence and proof of the apparition's existence or expose a prankster.

"I had made up my mind that the whole thing was a myth, but upon talking to one young man in whom I have considerable confidence, I decided that there was something back of all this talk and decided to make the trip to the cabin and camp a night or two," said Duckworth. "Guy Williams is the young man to whom I refer. He told me a story of a weeping woman he saw while he was out on a hunting trip a year or two ago. He camped two nights at the cabin. The first night, nothing happened, but the second night, he did get a glimpse of the apparition, enough of a look to satisfy him that the ghost walks there."

The men settled in, and since they had seen no ghost, they all soon fell fast asleep. That is, until one of the men, Ellis Rathburn, sprang from his bed, almost hysterical, jumping over two other men, Harry Byrd and Ray Hall, making his way toward the front door. He was in such a hurry that he got caught up in the camera and broke it.

"We were all convinced that the weeping woman ghost was there and not a joke," said Duckworth. Ralph Cuplin had sense enough to grab the second camera and quickly snap a photograph. The men were all satisfied that the weeping woman ghost was real, and they wrote up a notice, all signing it, and in their minds, the weeping woman ghost is 100 percent real.

# DANIEL HENNESSY MANSION

Just twenty miles outside of Anaconda lies a beautiful and majestic mansion at 847 West Park Street in Butte. Stories of ghostly apparitions being seen in the home's basement, stairs and kitchen are common. Many feel the ghost is the spirit of Daniel Hennessy himself.

Daniel Hennessy (1854–1908) was a self-made millionaire, originally born in New Brunswick, Canada. In 1879, when he was just twenty-five years old, he moved to Montana and began working for E.L. Bonner and Company. Soon, he dreamed of owning his own business, so he teamed up with Copper King Marcus Daly, who also believed in his vison. Soon, they opened a department store that had an unusual concept at the time: an all-in-one-stop shopping experience. The six-story department store was a place where a customer could buy anything

A very rare photograph of Daniel Hennessy. Over one thousand people came to his funeral from both Anaconda and Butte. *From the Butte-Silver Bow Public Archives, Butte, Montana; use was purchased by the author.*

from carpet to groceries. The store had seventeen departments and proudly employed over three hundred people. Inside the building, people were amazed at the expensive counters and staircases and rich surroundings. Daly and Hennessy felt shopping there should also be an experience. The upper floors of the Hennessy building became the headquarters for the Anaconda Company. More of Hennessy's Big Stores opened throughout Montana.

On August 24, 1897, Daniel (age forty-two) married a young woman named Mary Furlong (age twenty-nine) in Omaha, Nebraska. Mary was born in San Francisco, California, in 1865. They proceeded to have three children: Margaret (1869), Daniel Jr. (1901) and Paul (1906).

Daniel was determined to build a fantastic granite brick mansion in northwest Butte for his family. The 9,766-square-foot (not including the basement) Neo-Classical structure would boast eleven bedrooms, seven bathrooms and four fireplaces with hand-carved mahogany mantels, and it was a point of personal pride for local architect William O'Brien. It cost Hennessy $60,000 to build (about $2,020,302.27 today) his grand home. No expense was spared in the construction of this 13,000-square-foot home located on the corner of Park and Excelsior Streets. Among the earliest visitors to the Hennessy mansion was Admiral George Dewey, a hero of the Spanish-American War.

Unfortunately, Hennessy died suddenly in 1908, as he walked home from his department store. He was just fifty-three years old. His body lay in state

Daniel Hennessy's "big store" department in Butte, Montana, circa 1908. It was decorated with flags for the Fourth of July parade. *Library of Congress; Norman A. Forsyth, photographer.*

within the walls of his glorious mansion (in the parlor) on January 29 from 5:30 to 8:30 a.m. for loved ones to visit. The *Butte Miner* wrote, "For all who desire may look for the last time upon the face of the splendid citizen." Promptly at 9:30 a.m., the funeral procession of over one thousand people moved from the north on Excelsior Street, along to Granite Street and Idaho Street and then moved to Mercury Street until Hennessy's body was finally set down at St. Patrick's Church. The city was in such mourning over the loss of Hennessy that businesses, mines and even schools were closed in honor of him. Flags were flown at half-mast until the next day on order of Joseph Corby, the city's then-current mayor. Countless Anaconda citizens came to honor Hennessy, brought in by a special train.

Does Hennessy still roam the halls and rooms of his old stomping grounds, unable to leave his fabulous fortress in his beloved city of Butte?

*Note: Today, the home is a private residence. Please do not disturb the owners. Many photographs can be found online for the curious, including many magnificent interior photographs from when the home was listed for sale on Realtor.com.*

# WILLIAM CLARK MANSION

Nearby is another haunted mansion at 219 West Granite Street in Butte, built by another Montana Copper King. It is reportedly haunted by Senator William Andrews Clark (1839–1925) himself. His ghost offers a warm and welcoming presence, as if he is glad to see you and happy that you are there. Many see his shadowy figure or hear his soft footsteps. They home once served as a Catholic convent in the early 1900s. Since 1953, the beautiful Romanesque Revival Victorian structure has been operating as a bed-and-breakfast, privately owned, operated and occupied by the Cote family.

The fabulously wealthy William Clark poses for a rare photograph. *Library of Congress.*

The grand structure took four long years to complete at a cost of $260,000 ($7,861,312.24 in 2022). Clark, at the time, was considered one of the richest men in the world. Clark had a humble childhood, born into poverty in Pennsylvania in 1839. He was educated at a two-year law school in Iowa (though he never practiced) and then taught in Missouri for a year in 1859. He soon got adventurous and roamed to Colorado after catching wind about mining. He later moved to Bannock, Montana, to claim a grubstake (he later sold it for $1,500). With his meager profit, he purchased a horse team and wagon and began selling supplies to miners in mining camps. He realized his passion was not in mining itself but in making money off the hardworking miners. He then traveled to Salt Lake City, Utah, and Boise, Idaho, for a while. He put his law schooling to work when he began banking in Deer Lodge, repossessing mines, smelters, newspapers—anything he could get his hands on. A foreclosed mill was his biggest and best money-maker; milling ore for others was big money.

The practice of foreclosing on hardworking men while reeling in ridiculous amounts of money did not go over well with most folks. Mark Twain himself despised Clark and once said, "Clark was a rotten human being, a shame to the American nation and the most disgusting creature that the republic has produced since Tweed's time."

It is recorded that Clark began amassing a fortune, and at the time of the construction of his first mansion, he was earning the ridiculous sum of $17 million a month. How this humble teacher went from selling supplies to miners to become one of the richest men in the world is truly an incredible feat. He profited extensively from silver and copper mines and was soon elected to the Montana senate.

When he started the construction of his Butte mansion, it was said that the entire project cost him only half a day's income. His net worth in 1900 was over $50 million.

Clark spared no expense—he did not need to. His Butte palace had thirty-four rooms: a sixty-four-foot-long ballroom, a pool hall, a chapel, a library and nine fireplaces. It boasted Tiffany glass, muraled ceilings and hand-carved mantels and staircases (the staircase alone took four years to carve). The construction pursued nonstop from 1884 to 1888.

But to not mention Clark's continual excessive spending and other real estate ventures would not put his wealth into the right perspective. The humble, half-starving boy from Pennsylvania would accomplish and secure more fortune in his eighty-six years than is comprehensible. His wealth put Rockefeller and Carnegie to shame.

# "Clark's Folly": The Greatest Mansion New York Ever Saw!

In 1897, Clark decided he wanted to move to New York to build the grandest and most expensive mansion that New Yorkers would ever see. And he did just that. Unfortunately, after his death, the very same New Yorkers almost demanded the "eyesore" be torn down.

His megamansion took fourteen years to complete and cost over $7 million ($249,871,325 million in 2022) to build. His inspirations got so out of hand that in order to supply all of the stone needed, he had to purchase his own

The lavish Clark mansion on Fifth Avenue in New York City during the winter of 1905. It was torn down in 1925 to make room for apartments. *Library of Congress.*

quarry. If that wasn't enough, he later had to purchase a bronze foundry that employed two hundred men in order to furnish all the bronze embellishments needed for his vision. The castle was supplied with secret passageways, hidden doors and complicated stairways. Once completed, the home had 121 rooms (26 for the servants alone) and 32 bathrooms. One could easily get lost in all those rooms. Then, Clark had to build his own railway underground to supply the vast amount of coal needed to heat such a grand structure.

The mansion also boasted four art galleries, filled to the ceiling with very expensive collections. A swimming pool with Turkish baths, the oak transported from the Sherwood Forest in England and an overpriced, ginormous organ (the largest in America) that reached all the way to the ceiling were other spectacular features in his home. (Later, the organ was tossed into the swamp area near Queens, New York.)

Some believed Clark just could not spend his money fast enough—or be more ridiculous and arrogant. While some people were struggling to feed their families, Clark was hellbent on frivolously spending as much money as he could. Every aspect of the nine-story mansion was over the top—in every single square inch of the design.

Local New Yorkers called Senator William Clark's mansion on Fifth Avenue "Clark's Folly," because they felt it was an ugly eyesore. *Library of Congress.*

Two years after his death, in 1925, his widow, Anna Eugenia La Chapelle (just twenty-three years old) and daughter Huguette sold the home for just $3 million—a huge loss—to Anthony Campagna. The home was torn down in 1972 and sadly replaced with a standard apartment building.

If there was ever a place where a ghost is angry and haunting it, this site at 962 Fifth Avenue in the Upper East side of Manhattan is it! Clark poured a lot of his money, time and energy into building such a fabulous mansion. To think it just got torn down and replaced with commonplace apartments is unbelievable but true.

Perhaps *because* his New York City mansion was torn down, Clark's ghost feels the need to hang out in his original home, located in Butte, Montana.

Some claim the spirit of Elizabeth Boner Thompson can be heard dancing in the ballroom on the third floor of his mansion in Butte. (Elizabeth's mother, Sarah, was Clark's older sister. She died when Elizabeth was just seven years old and was raised by the Clark family.) Why in the world would a ghost girl ever want to leave such a grand and beautiful mansion?

*Note: For a good glimpse at interior and exterior photographs of "Clark's Folly," as New Yorkers called this ridiculous mansion, please visit https://www.historicalhomesofamerica.com/ post/clark-mansion-clark-s-folly-fifth-avenue-new-york-city or https://www.amusingplanet. com/2018/12/william-clarks-expensive-folly.html. Over fifty photographs of the mansion can be found at https://collections.mcny.org/C.aspx?VP3=SearchResult&VBID=24UAY W52YJ6TM&VP3=SearchResult&VBID=24UAYW52YJ6TM.*

# IN CONCLUSION

I am hoping the mixture of local history, architectural details, dates and figures and paranormal tales in my books continues to enrich readers' lives and encourage them to explore the various places revealed therein. Stories of ghosts, hauntings and restless spirits have been around for centuries, and they will continue until the end of time. Perhaps people are fascinated by spirits because they want some sort of proof that there is life after death; they desire to know their loved ones are not suffering. Others may simply think the paranormal is an interesting avenue to study.

As technology advances, the desire to capture proof of the existence of an afterlife has increased dramatically and is no longer limited to Ouija boards, crystal balls, tea leaves, psychics and slate writers. People no longer frown on those who choose to believe in ghosts and the spirit world; in the past, most thought it was all hoaxes and make-believe. It is now common to hear conversations about ghosts and spirits almost everywhere you go. Hundreds of paranormal groups are popping up all over the place, their members eager to prove the existence of ghosts and visit haunted places.

I am glad to have many teachers and parents thank me for my books and tell me that they cannot get their children to take the time to read or even have the slightest interest in learning about history but that my books have opened the door for both of these things. I was once told that there was a waitlist with over seventy-six students who were waiting for my book at the local library—for that, I am proud and happy.

And as locals and tourists roam in and out of Anaconda stores and structures or enjoy a libation in an old hotel or bar, I hope that they find these tales from the past fascinating, frightening and intriguing. I also hope this book makes them stop in the entryways of mansions and think of the pioneers who built them. When they walk through old buildings and cemeteries, I hope they ponder the past and possibly take my book with them as they search the local graves. Maybe they will pause for just a second or two to remember those early miners and proprietors who worked so hard to create the wonderful towns in *Haunted Southwested Montana*.

Better yet, I hope my readers get the eerie chance to experience an EVP, see or capture an apparition on camera or feel the creepy touch of a ghostly hand against their skin.

Happy hauntings!

# BIBLIOGRAPHY

## WEBSITES

Ancestry. www.ancestry.com.
Dumas Brothel. "History of the Dumas." www.dumas-brothel.com/history-of-the-dumas-2/.
Find a Grave. www.findagrave.com.
Legends of America. "Henry Plummer—Sheriff Meets a Noose." www.legendsofamerica.com/mt-henryplummer/.
———. "Innocents Gang of Montana." www.legendsofamerica.com/innocents-gang/.
Library of Congress. www.loc.gov.
MTGenWeb. "Mining History of Beaverhead County." www.mtgenweb.com/beaverhead/mining/mininghistory.htm.
Murderpedia. www.murderpedia.org.
My Itchy Travel Feet. "Bannack Ghost Town Is a Step Back in Time." www.myitchytravelfeet.com/relive-gold-rush-history-bannack-ghost-town/.
Visit Southwest Montana. "Grant-Kohrs Ranch." www.southwestmt.com/ghosts/ghost-stories/grant-kohrs-ranch/.
———. "Southwest Montana Ghost Stories." www. southwestmt.com/ghosts/ghost-stories/.

## ANACONDA STANDARD

*Anaconda Standard*. November 8, 1890.
————. February 28, 1896.
————. July 1, 1896.
————. December 12, 1898.
————. December 18, 1898.
————. January 9, 1899.
————. January 17, 1899.
————. May 23, 1899.
————. September 5, 1899.
————. December 31, 1899.
————. March 12, 1901.
————. March 17, 1901.
————. April 11, 1901.
————. April 14, 1904.
————. April 2, 1909.

## HENRY PLUMMER AND BANNACK, MONTANA

*Anaconda Standard*. January 11, 1892.
————. August 30, 1895.
Baumler, Ellen. "Bannack: A Spirited Town." *Ravalli Republic*, September 22, 2006.
*Butte Miner*. June 3, 1897.
*Madisonian*. February 10, 1894.
*Montana Standard*. August 8, 1954.
Pierce, Ben. "History Comes Alive in Montana's First Territorial Capital." *Montana Standard*, March 19, 2015.

## WORLEY

*Anaconda Standard*. February 21, 1897.
————. February 22, 1897.
————. February 23, 1897.
————. February 24, 1897.
————. September 2, 1897.

# GAGNER

*Anaconda Standard*. November 22, 1921.
————. October 28, 1923.
*Butte Miner*. December 1, 1921.
————. January 13, 1922.
————. July 14, 1922.
————. July 19, 1922.
*Great Falls Tribune*. January 13, 1922.
*Independent Record*. December 21, 1922.

# SHEPPARD

*Anaconda Standard*. January 17, 1899.
————. January 22, 1899.

# MCGEARY

*Butte Miner*. July 2, 1902.

# MONTANA STATE PRISON

*Great Falls Tribune*. April 20, 1959.
————. December 8, 1966.
*Milwaukie Journal*. February 23, 1968.
*Montana Standard*. April 17, 1959.
————. April 19, 1959.
Wikipedia. "Montana State Prison, 1959 Riot." https://en.wikipedia.org/
    wiki/Montana_State_Prison#1959_Riot.

# SHOEBOX ANNIE

*Helena Dependent*. May 6, 1933.
*Helper Journal*. May 12, 1938.
*Journal Times*. March 29, 1936.

*Montana Standard.* May 6, 1938.
————. May 7, 1938.
*Pittsburg Sun Telegraph.* April 15, 1945.
*St. Louis Dispatch.* July 25, 1935.

## Dorothy Dunn

*Anaconda Standard.* December 30, 1906.
*Butte Miner.* August 5, 1916.
————. August 8, 1916.
*Great Falls Tribune.* August 5, 1916.
————. October 19, 1930.
Haunted Houses. www.hauntedhouses.com.
Only in Your State. www.onlyinyourstate.com.

## Dumas Brothel

*Montana Standard.* February 23, 1991.
————. September 7, 2013.

## Dan Lucey

*Anaconda Standard.* June 30, 1899.
————. February 3, 1901.
————. March 17, 1901.

## Daily Missoulian

*Daily Missoulian.* July 30, 1917.

## Turkey Pete

Chapin, Peter. "The Convict Who Owned the World." *Montana Standard,*
    March 6, 1982.

Ecke, Richard. "The Charm of Turkey Pete." *Great Falls Tribune*, December 13, 1981.

## Anaconda Road Massacre

Raye, Janet. "Second Bloody Wednesday Victim Dead." *Hellraisers Journal*, December 9, 2020.

## Garnet Ghost Town and Granite County

Atlas Obscura. "Granit Ghost Town." https://www.atlasobscura.com/places/granite-ghost-town.

*Butte Miner*. April 21, 1912.

Daily Kos. "Garnet Ghost Town: Davey's Store (Photo Diary)." https://www.dailykos.com/stories/2018/8/8/1786659/-Garnet-Ghost-Town-Davey-s-Store-Photo-Diary.

Haunted Places. "Garnet Ghost Town." https://www.hauntedplaces.org/item/garnet-ghost-town/.

*Helena Herald*. October 4, 1912.

*Helena Independent*. October 4, 1912.

Montana Fish, Wildlife and Parks. "Granite Ghost Town State Park." https://fwp.mt.gov/stateparks/granite-ghost-town.

Past Prologue. "Garnet Ghost Town, Montana 1895–1948." http://dmarlin.com/pastprologue/blog/garnet-ghost-town-montana/. (This site has an excellent and extensive collection of photographs of Garnet.)

Western Mining History. "Garnet, Montana." https://westernmininghistory.com/towns/montana/garnet.

## Sand Park Cemetery

*Anaconda Standard*. September 27, 1898.

———. September 1, 1900.

———. November 27, 1901.

*Butte Daily Post*. March 17, 1898.

*Butte Miner*. May 28, 1893, September 24, 1907.

*Independent Review*. May 21, 1898.

*Missoulian.* December 8, 1907.
———. June 14, 1943.
*Philipsburg Mail.* April 29, 1898.

# Virginia City

Buchanan, Carol. "The Vigilantes of Montana, Part 7." Swan Range. https://www.carol-buchanan.com/vigilante/vigilantes7.html.
Haunted Places. "Haunted Places in Virginia City, Montana." https://www.hauntedplaces.org/virginia-city-mt/.
Virginia City and Nevada City, Montana. https://www.virginiacitymt.com/.

# Miscellaneous Websites

Discover Mining History with the Mining History Association. "2011 Mining History Association Field Trip." http://www.mininghistoryassociation.org/Philipsburg.htm.
Haunted Places. "Haunted Places in Anaconda, Montana." https://www.hauntedplaces.org/anaconda-mt/.
Travel. "Phantom of the Opera: 10 Haunted Theaters Throughout the World." https://www.thetravel.com/haunted-theaters-throughout-world.
Waymarking. "City Hall Ghost Moves: Anaconda, MT." https://www.waymarking.com/waymarks/wmZD4K_CITY_HALL_GHOST_MOVES_Anaconda_MT.
———. "Opera House Theatre: Philipsburg, MT." https://www.waymarking.com/waymarks/wm109V7_Opera_House_Theatre_Philipsburg_MT.

# Clark Mansion

Copper King Mansion. http://thecopperkingmansion.com/.

## HENNESSY MANSION

Haunted Houses. "Haunted Locations in Butte, Montana." https://hauntedhouses.com/category/montana/butte/.

## VARIOUS ANACONDA LANDMARKS

LandmarkHunter.com. "Deer Lodge County, Montana." https://landmarkhunter.com/mt/deer-lodge/.

## BRIDGET SULLIVAN/LIZZIE BORDEN

*Anaconda Standard*. October 19, 1902.

DyingWords.net. "Did Lizzie Borden Really Ax-Murder Her Parents?" http://dyingwords.net/tag/bridget-sullivan/.

Miller, Sarah. "11 'Facts' About Lizzie Borden Debunked." Criminal Element. January 12, 2016. https://www.criminalelement.com/11-facts-about-lizzie-borden-debunked-sarah-miller-murders-trial-of-the-century-forty-whacks/.

*Montana Standard*. December 30, 1928.

Record Click. "A Genealogist Gets Details and Grusome Clues in the Lizzie Borden, Bridget Sullivan Case." https://www.recordclick.com/a-genealogist-gets-details-and-gruesome-clues-in-the-lizzie-borden-bridget-sullivan-case/.

Ross, Jerry. "Bridget Sullivan: After Fall River." Hatchet, July 16, 2018. https://lizzieandrewborden.com/HatchetOnline/bridget-sullivan-after-fall-river.html.

## CROSS COUNTRY PARANORMAL INVESTIGATIONS WITH BENJAMIN YOUNG

Email: CrossCountryParanormal@gmail.com
Website: www.ccpinvestigations.com
Facebook: www.facebook.com/crosscountryparanormal
Facebook Group: www.facebook.com/groups/crosscountryparanormal
YouTube: www.youtube.com/crosscountryparanormaltv

# ABOUT THE AUTHOR

Originally from Upstate New York, Deborah Cuyle loves everything about the history of America's cities—large or small. She has also written: *Haunted Snohomish* (WA), *Ghostly Tales of Snohomish* (WA), *Haunted Everett* (WA), *Ghosts of Leavenworth and the Cascade Foothills* (WA), *Ghosts of Coeur d'Alene and the Silver Valley* (ID), *Ghosts and Legends of Spokane* (WA), *Ghostly Tales of the Pacific Northwest* (OR, WA and BC), *Wicked Coeur d'Alene* (ID), *Wicked Spokane* (WA), *Murder and Mayhem in Coeur d'Alene and the Silver Valley* (ID), *Murder and Mayhem in Spokane* (WA), *Kidding Around Portland* (OR), *Images of Cannon Beach* (OR) and *The 1910 Wellington Disaster* (WA). Her other passions include volunteering at her local historical society, rescuing animals, exploring museums, rock hunting and horses. She, her husband and her son are currently remodeling a haunted, crumbling mansion in Milbank, South Dakota, that was built in 1883 and was once a funeral home.

*Visit us at*
www.historypress.com